ACKNOWLEDGEMENTS

THE LONDON SCHOOL OF ECONOMICS AND POLITICAL SCIENCE STUDENT'S UNION (LSESU) AMNESTY INTERNATIONAL SOCIETY AND THE EDITOR OF THIS JOURNAL WOULD LIKE TO THANK THE LSE ANNUAL FUND FOR THEIR GENEROSITY, WITHOUT WHICH THE PUBLICATION OF THIS JOURNAL WOULD NOT HAVE BEEN POSSIBLE.

ADDITIONAL THANKS TO

ALL WHO HAVE CONTRIBUTED THEIR WORK TO THIS JOURNAL AND THE COMMITTEE OF THE LSESU AMNESTY INTERNATIONAL SOCIETY 2012-2013.

ABOUT THE LSESU AMNESTY INTERNATIONAL SOCIETY

THE LSESU AMNESTY INTERNATIONAL SOCIETY HAS THE MOST MEMBERS OF ANY UNIVERSITY AMNESTY INTERNATIONAL SOCIETY IN THE UK. IT WAS FORMED OVER A DECADE AGO AND HAS SINCE BECOME ONE OF THE LARGEST CAMPAIGN GROUPS AT LSE. IT ALSO FACILITATES CAMPAIGNS IN CONJUNCTION WITH AMNESTY INTERNATIONAL SOCIETIES THROUGHOUT THE UNIVERSITY OF LONDON.

OUR MISSION

OUR MISSION IS TO ENGAGE WITH THE STUDENTS OF THE UNIVERSITY IN ORDER TO PROMOTE THE VALUES OF AMNESTY INTERNATIONAL, IN PROTECTING INDIVIDUALS WHEREVER JUSTICE, FREEDOM AND OTHER HUMAN RIGHTS ARE DENIED. THROUGH CAMPAIGNING, FUNDRAISING AND PUBLICATIONS, WE SEEK TO RAISE AWARENESS OF HUMAN RIGHTS VIOLATIONS, AND TO WORK TOWARD THEIR PREVENTION.

EDITOR:
ELIZABETH STOUT

FRONT AND BACK COVER DESIGN:
JAMIE PELLING

All enquiries should be sent to:
Justitia Omnibus Human Rights Journal
LSE Amnesty International Society
c/o LSE Students' Union
East Building, Houghton Street
London
WC2A 2AE
United Kingdom

www.fast-print.net/store.php

Justitia Omnibus

ISBN: 978-178035-638-9

A catalogue record for this book is available from the British Library

First published 2013 by
FASTPRINT PUBLISHING
Peterborough, England.

An environmentally friendly book printed and bound in England by www.printondemand-worldwide.com

This book is made entirely of chain-of-custody materials

CONTENTS

Foreword

Elizabeth Stout
Editor (2012 - 2013)

Welcome to the third volume of the *Justitia Omnibus,* the annual human rights journal of the Students' Union Amnesty International Society at the London School of Economics and Political Science.

To celebrate the 65th Anniversary of the Universal Declaration of Human Rights, this volume is dedicated to the 30 Articles set out in this Declaration. To this end, this volume features a piece on each Article of the Universal Declaration. These raise many issues surrounding the Declaration, and its function in today's society. They ask questions such as: how are our rights fulfilled to different extents in different countries across the world? Who bears the brunt of these violations? How can we work towards the further achievement of these rights? And how relevant is the Universal Declaration 65 years after its creation? Taken together, this journal helps to illustrate how our rights are being fulfilled in 2013.

2013 has been a significant year for human rights. History was made when, in March 2013, the first ever Arms Trade Treaty was signed at the UN General Assembly (see page 75). That there were but three abstentions to the Treaty will hopefully come to illustrate a renewed commitment to the achievement of human rights for all. However, 2013 has also been significant for human rights in a more negative sense. Human rights violations such as forced disappearances continue as a result of the conflict in Syria (see page 59). In the UK, suggestions were made of a temporary withdrawal from the European Convention on Human Rights to secure the extradition of Abu Qatada. Investigations into attitudes toward rape in India revealed that many believed the victims were to blame (see page 43). A Swiss cyclist became another victim of gang rape in India. These violations occur, unfortunately, alongside many other systematic and unyielding violations across the globe.

Volume Three of the *Justitia Omnibus* seeks to raise awareness of such violations. The distance yet to travel in the achievement of our human rights must be recognised. It is the hope of both the Editor and those who have contributed to this volume that the issues raised in this journal will help to facilitate this recognition. It may then, alongside the many policy changes recommended throughout the journal, assist in moving us further toward the realisation of our rights.

C.M.K. DJORDJEVIC

PREAMBLE
THE KINGDOM YET TO COME

"Whereas disregard and contempt for human rights have resulted in barbarous acts which have outraged the conscience of mankind, and the advent of a world in which human beings shall enjoy freedom of speech and belief and freedom from fear and want has been proclaimed as the highest aspiration of the common people,"

An idea is becoming increasingly prevalent among intellectuals today - most especially American ones.[1] The idea, quite succinctly put, is that technological progress leads to - perhaps even causes? - moral progress. Thus, genocide, say, is not something that occurs in modern nations. It is a strange relic of the past that is merely a symptom of unscientific culture that capitalism and free trade will surely fix eventually. This idea would be hilarious were it not so dangerous.

Why hilarious? Because it is espoused by a group who, not even a century ago, engaged in such a violent and apocalyptic death struggle that it wrecked an entire civilization. Because the only thing that ended this struggle was the rising of two man made demonic suns whose awful light incinerated Japanese cities. Because what we can still hear from the horrid death camps is the screams of people who had become numbers-bureaucratically reduced and scientifically dealt with.[2] This very civilization is now saying - yet again, once more! - that progress in knowledge is progress in morals. An absurdly laughable claim for anyone with even a passing knowledge of history.

Why dangerous? Because it makes human rights, a true achievement of our times, nothing but 'common sense.' Because it says that our perspective must be the 'right' one. Because it makes dictators and war an abnormality when, truth be told, they are the commonality of human history.[3]

The Universal Declaration on human rights begins with an acknowledgment that the denial of such things as human dignity and freedom are the root causes of systematic killings of human beings. It, unlike so much of what is prevalent today, realizes that this recognition is profoundly revolutionary, precarious and, above all, in deep need of constant vigilance.

What I want to argue for in this brief piece is the need for constant vigilance. As has been said, many times before and in many modalities, evil triumphs when good people do nothing. In many ways, then, this piece is a call to arms for those who want to preserve human rights and human dignity. We shall discuss why, first, mere technological prowess isn't enough to ground human rights. Then we shall look to history and find our kingdom of human rights not seen anywhere. Finally, I shall argue that the kingdom is yet to come - in the most important sense of the term.

---

1 A glance at US "intellectual" literature shows this trend. Thus we have, for instance, *Angels of Our Better Nature* by S. Pinker. The basic arguments in this, and other books of its ilk, are simply that an integrated world-capitalist market will, eventually, preclude wars as wars tend to be "bad for business" (disregarding the vast sums of money the US invests in its own military, of course).

2 H. Arendt explores the concept of "evil as Banality" beautifully in her classic work *Eichmann and the Holocaust*

3 Since Herodotus, history has been, in many respects, the history of war and violence.

"And Ye Shall be as gods." The failure of Technology:

What did the world realize at the end of the second world war? What died in the camps besides around 9 million people? What was burned to ashes with the utter annihilation of Nagasaki and Hiroshima?

What we lost, really, was a myth. The myth, spelled out and discarded by a generation of thinkers who, in some real sense, never truly overcame the horror they saw[4], was that technology was salvation. The argument is quite simple; (a) all wars are fought over the scarcity of resources - from tribes clashing with each other in pre-history right down to the present (b) technology promises us a way to create a near infinite supply of resources, ergo, (c) technology will stop wars.

The European experience shows that all three of these premises are wrong. (a) The killing of Jewish people, Romas, Slavs, homosexuals and other 'undesirables' doesn't seem to have much to do with scarcity of resources. Further, World War One seems to prove that pride, as much as anything else, can be a reason for war. World War One was not about resources, at least not ostensibly. It was about how a newly unified Germany under the brilliant leadership of Bismark (who was sacked a few years before the war began) threatened to destabilize power. Maybe in some abstract sense power is a resource. But certainly it is not the same as the hunter-gathering tribes who fight over a valuable game site.

(b) The best refutation for the idea that salvation will come from the machines is a quote by Oppenheimer that is very close to my heart "We knew the world would not be the same. A few people laughed. A few cried. Most people were silent. I remembered the line from the Hindu scripture, the Bhagavad gita. Vishnu is trying to persuade the Prince [Arjuna] that he should do his duty and, to impress him, takes on his multi-armed form and says 'now I have become death. The destroyer of worlds' I suppose we all thought that, one way or another."[5] To extend the metaphor, our technology can be a glorious companion on the path towards a wondrous garden of earthly pleasures but it can also become death, the possibility of utterly annihilating ourselves in a way unheard of before.

(c) This can be quite simply refuted by a look at history up to now. Did technological progress stop the US-Korean war? The pogroms in central Asia after the fall of the USSR? The various coups and counter-coups in Africa and South America? Has it given us anything more that a more effective way to kill others? It seems to me that the only truthful answer to these questions is no.

It would do well here to recall the line that tempted Adam in Genesis - you shall be as gods. Truly, horrifically, who can argue against the fact that such a prophetic statement has not come to pass with truly earth shattering repercussions?

---

4 E. Levinas, J. Derrida, E. Wiesel, C. Milosz and, to some extent, R. Opinhiemer all seemed to express the same fundamental doubts.

5 J. Robert Opinhimer on the Trinity test, 1965

C.M.K. Djordjevic

"The Strong do as they will and the weak suffer what they must." The weight of history

Until very recently, perhaps until the last century in fact, this line was the guiding line for state-craft. From the Ottoman policies in the Balkans to the French ones in North Africa, from the Japanese way of "handling" the Chinese in the second world war to the US's "noble" support of dictators to keep the world safe from communism, this passage fairly well sums up human history.

In a wonderful story, Pompey the great - the main "defender" of the Roman Republic from Caesar - laid siege to a Roman city during the course of the civil war. The inhabitants, being Roman citizens one and all, dispatched a lawyer to argue that the siege was completely illegal and that Pompey should "cease and desist" at once. After several hours with the lawyer, Pompey exclaimed, exasperated and extremely tired of legal mumbo-jumbo, "stop quoting laws to us - we, who have the swords!"

An example that is not nearly as distant historically, but reflects the same spirit, is the US supreme court's *Worcester v. Georgia.* The state of Georgia wanted to, in effect, incorporate some land that was held by the native Americans. The court, under Justice Marshall, ruled that Georgia had no right to the land and that it should "cease and desist" any attempt to expropriate the land. President Jackson's hauntingly laconic reply was "John Marshall made his decision, now let him go enforce it." And, as to the question of the native Americans, "build a fire under them. When it gets hot enough, they'll go."

In both cases, we see something that Thucydides in his *History of the Peloponnesian War* saw with painful clarity as the war between Athens and Sparta dragged on: human laws and customs are, in a very deep sense, conventions we live by. And when those of us with swords have other ideas, things go horribly wrong.

The need for ideals

With these lessons in mind, we have a clear view of the problem at hand. The weight of history seems to argue against human rights. And technology seems to provide no help. It is a trope, but a fundamental one, that history is written in blood. And yet, I still believe that the human rights project can succeed.

To paraphrase Pascal, humanity is but the weakest of reeds in nature - so much less robust than some of nature's other creates - but humanity is a thinking one. We have built wonders that, even 50 years ago, were unthinkable. We have seen cities rise in forbidden lands, swamps and lakes drained, the birth of an entirely new world, so called cyberspace, and the spread of information in a way unprecedented. Humanity can think.

And thinking, in some deep sense, is envisioning things that aren't. Perhaps even envisioning the impossible (who would think that humans would take to the skies one day?) It is this ability to idealize, to invent the world and ourselves anew, that seems like it is our best hope.

To look for human rights in the triumphant growth of neo-liberal capitalism is deeply flawed.[6] Equally flawed is the attempt to look for human rights in the progress of science or the history of humanity. Human rights are of a strange class of things whose history shall always belong to the future. Yet far from bemoaning this, I merely remind the reader that striving for this new world is our duty and our blessing. Yet we must never forget that human rights, like all ideals, only work as long as we strive and struggle for them. Without that, they are but another gesture on the pages of the blood soaked history of the homo sapien.

6 P. O'Connell, 'On Reconciling Irreconcilables: Neo-liberal Globalisation and Human Rights' is a great place to look at why.

CLARA BLAMBERGER

ARTICLE 1
WHERE IS OUR BROTHERHOOD?

> *"All human beings are born free and equal in dignity and rights. They are endowed with reason and conscience and should act towards one another in a spirit of brotherhood."*

"Of all the evils for which man has made himself responsible, none is so degrading, so shocking or so brutal as his abuse of the better half of humanity; the female sex (not the weaker sex)." – Mahatma Gandhi, 1921

What would Mahatma Gandhi say, if he could see Indian society now? A society, in which about 12 million female foetuses have been killed in the last 3 decades,[1] only because they are girls – so that now the sex ratio is 914 women for every 1000 men[2]. A society, in which rape increased by 9.2% in 2011, kidnapping by 19.4% and torture by 5.8%[3]. And a society, in which each hour two women are raped,[4] and every 93 minutes a woman is killed[5]. In which 52% of adolescent girls and 57% of boys think it is justifiable that women are beaten in marriage[6].

India is the world's fourth most dangerous country for women – only after Afghanistan, the Democratic Republic of the Congo and Pakistan[7]. It ranks 134th of 187 countries in a 2011 UN index on women in politics, female education and employment, and sexual and maternal health – behind Saudi Arabia, Iraq and China[8]. Among all G20 countries, it is, moreover, the worst country for women to live in – again behind Saudi Arabia.[9]

---

[1] "Millions of female foetuses aborted in India." *The Telegraph*, 24 May 2011. Web. 8 April 2013. <http://www.telegraph.co.uk/news/worldnews/asia/india/8532190/Millions-of-female-foetuses-aborted-in-India.html>.

[2] Ghosh, Palash R. "Selective Abortion Of Female Fetuses In India Creating Gender Imbalance Crisis." *International Business Times*, 19 September 2012. Web. 8 April 2013. <http://www.ibtimes.com/selective-abortion-female-fetuses-india-creating-gender-imbalance-crisis-793298>.

[3] India. Ministry of Home Affairs. National Crime Records Bureau. *Crime in India 2011.* 28 June 2012. Web. 8 April 2013. <http://ncrb.nic.in/CD-CII2011/cii-2011/Chapter%205.pdf> .

[4] Khazan, Olga "How India's rape name-and-shame database could backfire." *The Washington Post*, 28 December 2012. Web. 8 April 2013. <http://www.washingtonpost.com/blogs/worldviews/wp/2012/12/28/how-indias-rape-name-and-shame-database-could-backfire/>.

[5] *Women and Drug Abuse: The Problem in India.* Rep. United Nations International Drug Control Program and Ministry of Social Justice and Empowerment, 6 May 2003. Web. 8 April 2013. <https://www.unodc.org/pdf/india/publications/women_Book-6-5-03/09_statusofwomeninindia.pdf>.

[6] Pidd, Helen. "Why is India so Bad for Women." *The Guardian,* 23 July 2012. Web. 8 April 2013. <http://www.guardian.co.uk/world/2012/jul/23/why-india-bad-for-women>.

[7] Bowcott, Owen. "Afghanistan Worst Place in World for Women, but India in Top Five." *The Guardian,* 15 June 2011. Web. 8 April 2013. <http://www.guardian.co.uk/world/2011/jun/15/worst-place-women-afghanistan-india> accessed 8/4/2013.

[8] "Rape and Murder in Delhi." *The Economist,* 5 January 2013. Web. 8 April 2013. <http://www.economist.com/news/leaders/21569031-horrible-attack-could-prove-turning-point-indias-women-rape-and-murder-delhi>.

[9] "India Ranked 'Worst' G-20 Country to be a Woman; Canada Declared the Best." *International Business Times: Traveller.* Web. 8 April 2013. <http://www.ibtimes.co.in/articles/352199/20120614/india-worst-country-woman-canada-best-saudi.htm>.

Article I of the Universal Declaration of Human Rights says: "All human beings are born free and equal in dignity and rights. They are endowed with reason and conscience and should act towards one another in a spirit of brotherhood."

This is only an illusion. Not all human beings are born free and equal – indeed, a major part of the world's population is not: women. And a great part of the population certainly does not act towards brotherhood either – otherwise, why would there be so much discrimination against what Gandhi described as the "better half of humanity"?

What has happened in India last December – the brutal gang rape of a 23-year old student[10], which has shocked the world – has only begun to put into perspective women's suffering – not just in Indian society, but all over the world. It illustrates the work to be done on gender equality and women's rights.

Women – in general – are born neither free nor equal in dignity and rights. Yes, the situation has improved for women (for example, access to primary education[11]), but still, all over the world, they are denied access to the health and education system; to secure employment; to property rights; credit; have only poor access to land. Women are, above all, victims of violence, especially during conflict, where rape is used as a weapon – as in Africa,[12] or Latin America before.[13] They are victims of human trafficking, genital mutilation and child marriage. 70% of the world's poor are women[14]. Even in developed countries, there are problems, for instance in equal payment. On average within the EU, the wage gap between women and men is at 16%[15]. Women only play a small role in politics too - the number of female leaders of states remains a very far cry from half of the 193 states in the world. The average percentage of women in parliaments is 19.5%[16] - they are, thus, outnumbered 1 to 4. Conflict solutions and peace building is another point where women are greatly underrepresented.

What are the reasons for this inequality? Hierarchies within societies, cultural and religious barriers, traditions that are historically deeply engraved in society and discrimination.

And what would possible solutions be? Above all, security and protection; countries need to create a legal framework which equally includes men and women. The social welfare system needs to equally protect women too, for example, when it comes to

---

[10] Burke, Jason. "Delhi Gang-Rape Accused Face Rape and Murder Charges." *The Guardian,* 3 January 2013. Web. 8 April 2013. <http://www.guardian.co.uk/world/2013/jan/03/delhi-gang-rape-accused-murder-charges>.

[11] *Beijing Platform for Action.* Rep. United Nations Documents, September 1995. Web. 8 April 2013. <http://www.un-documents.net/bpa-4-b.htm> accessed 8/4/2013.

[12] Smith-Spark, Laura. "How Did Rape Become a Weapon of War?" *BBC News.* Web. 8 April 2013. <http://news.bbc.co.uk/1/hi/4078677.stm>

[13] Ibid

[14] "Women and Poverty" *Global Poverty Info Bank.* Web. 8 April 2013. <http://www.globalpovertyproject.com/infobank/women>.

[15] *Gender Pay Gap Statistics.* Rep. European Commission, March 2013. Web. 8 April 2013. <http://epp.eurostat.ec.europa.eu/statistics_explained/index.php/Gender_pay_gap_statistics>.

[16] "International Women's Day 2012: Women's Representation in Politics." *The Guardian,* March 2012. Web. 8 April 2013. <http://www.guardian.co.uk/news/datablog/2012/mar/07/women-representation-in-politics-worldwide>.

the healthcare system, where women all over the world are often discriminated against. Next, education is central – without education, there can be no economic or political empowerment of women; and, more importantly, no removal of those cultural barriers which prevent women from actively participating in society. When it comes to employment, women must have access to the labour market. For rural women, for example, training sessions can be introduced; as well as for women who would want to stand in political elections: local and national. Only when women are empowered, can there be progress in a society; in the development of an economy. It is smart economics[17] to include women in a country's economy; it is also proven that children of women who are educated are more likely to go to school[18] – meaning life for future generations will improve too.

Women's rights have been promoted for a long time and the data and solutions brought up in this article have been discussed before – so why do we still talk about it, why is it still important? Because people, apparently, do not listen – there is no "act towards one another in the spirit of brotherhood." And as long as people do not take it seriously and do not act, as long as they do not listen to what is said about women's suffering, so we must continue the discussion. Article I of the Universal Declaration of Human Rights seems so simple - yet why, then, is it so difficult to achieve, why do we not act towards it? It is deserved by everyone; perhaps women above all, who have suffered too long.

---

[17] *Inequalities and Multiple Discrimination in Access to Healthcare.* Rep. European Union Agency for Fundamental Rights. 2011. Web. 11 April 2013. <http://fra.europa.eu/sites/default/files/fra_uploads/1421-Multiple-discrimination_Factsheet_EN.pdf>.

[18] Morales, Zia. "Empowering Women is Smart Economics." Web log post. *The World Bank,* 15 October 2012. Web. 11 April 2013. <http://blogs.worldbank.org/psd/empowering-women-is-smart-economics>.

VINCE HARROLD

ARTICLE 2
THINKING CRITICALLY ABOUT THE UNIVERSAL DECLARATION OF HUMAN RIGHTS

"Everyone is entitled to all the rights and freedoms set forth in this Declaration, without distinction of any kind, such as race, colour, sex, language, religion, political or other opinion, national or social origin, property, birth or other status. Furthermore, no distinction shall be made on the basis of the political, jurisdictional or international status of the country or territory to which a person belongs, whether it be independent, trust, non-self-governing or under any other limitation of sovereignty."

"Then I noticed a small sketch in oils, on a panel, representing a woman, draped and blindfolded, carrying a lighted torch" - Joseph Conrad

The meaning of Article 2 of the Universal Declaration of Human Rights (UDHR) is eponymous in essence: it is a formulation of the simple vision of the declaration to detail a set of rights that are universal, to whom "everyone is entitled...without distinction of any kind". The right to life, liberty, and security of person. The freedom from slavery, servitude, torture and degrading behaviour. Few today would argue against the universality of these rights to the human person. Nevertheless, neither the formulation or the implementation of the rights of the UDHR can be said to be truly holistic. Moreover, I go so far as to argue that the UDHR represents a threat to the attainment of equal and universal justice when its narrow thirty articles are conflated with a complete and incontestable account of human rights.

Perhaps the most fruitful point of departure in discussing the UDHR is acknowledging that rights change. That is to say, rights are accepted and rejected over time and across societies. Even universal rights change when considered in this respect. The right to life and liberty may be timeless, but its species-wide acknowledgement is recent and incomplete. The same can be said of rights to democracy or against torture. Whether or not such rights are endemic to the human person by way of his or her very existence, their acknowledgement must be viewed as historically and culturally conditioned.

Two key observations follow from the relativity of rights suggested above. The first is to recognise that agreement over the statement of rights does not equate to agreement over the interpretation of those same rights, including their weight and value. The second is that any such list of universal rights is not complete. A universal statement on human rights made no more than two hundred years ago would not have included the freedom from slavery for all peoples of the world. Such a statement would be viewed today as incomplete. In this respect, the UDHR should be celebrated as a historical achievement for its global codification of rights previously unacknowledged. Through this act, the UDHR marks a momentous occasion in the process of struggle for the emancipation of humankind. Nevertheless, there is no reason to expect that our contemporary conceptualisation of human rights is any less limited by an historical relativity of thought.

Therefore, the challenge for human rights comes in thinking critically about the UDHR. There is an overwhelming temptation to equate the achievement of the formulations of the declaration as a panacea for global injustice. Certainly, their fulfillment would mark an unprecedented move towards this goal and the fight for the universal enjoyment of the most basic liberties and interests is more than worthy. Nevertheless, the attainment of these elementary human needs is not an end result but a stepping stone. Indeed, there is a great danger in equating these positions. The UDHR holds a focus on preventing cruelty and violence in its most specific, often physical, forms. Certainly, the Western-liberal advocacy for the inherent rights of the individual are beyond admirable. However, the same system's generation of social inequality and moral apathy need to be challenged in an equally strong manner. The consequence of overlooking oppression at a systemic level - a system we create, inhabit and sustain - is to allow a far more subtle but equally insidious form of injustice to persist.

In the concluding remarks of this article I wish to return to the message of its epigraph. Our journey towards a world of equity and justice may be better lit by the UDHR, but the path remains obscured. There are still blindfolds left to remove.

JAMIE PELLING

ARTICLE 3
LADY JUSTICE

"Everyone has the right to life, liberty and security of person."

This image embodies the constant struggle in protecting the rights guaranteed in Article 3. The legal system must be the guard of the right to 'life liberty, and security of person' and here, Lady Justice is facing a cloudy sky which embodies the dappled nature of this right around the world. There are periods of blue sky, but there is always the possibility of cloud. Yet Lady Justice continues to face this challenge, despite its seemingly interminable threat.

ARTICLE 4
JAMILA

"No one shall be held in slavery or servitude; slavery and the slave trade shall be prohibited in all their forms."

My name is Jamila, synonymous to beautiful,
If only my life had turned out that way.

I was living my ordinary life when they came,

Hooded men claiming to be friends,

They kidnapped me and poured white sticky powder in my nose and mouth,

The sickly smell, the beating hands, mouths moving, words not reaching.

Then came the shouts and the tugging as I was handed over like a dishcloth,

To a man who was a monster, always hitting, never stopping.

Stains on my hands from the labor during the day,

Stains on the bed from abuse during the night.

I would wake up every morning feeling that the day would be my last,

For this is my story; is it a life, is it worth living?

Many think of slavery as an old problem; one of slave ships carrying people half way around the world to lands they didn't even know existed. The truth is that it is estimated that almost 21 million people work in forced labour today, the majority of which is represented by women and girls.[1] An example of such slavery is in India, which has, by some estimates, the world's largest number of slaves[2]. Here, an increasing number of women and girls are sold into marriage every year. Women and young girls are sold for as little as $120 to men who often burden them with strenuous labour and abuse them.[3] According to the founder of a grassroots organisation aiming to find bride traffickers and their victims, "the girls do equal amounts of work in two jobs. They are sex slaves, not just to one man but a group of 10 or 12 men. Apart from that there is agriculture - working on the farms with

---

1 International Labour Organization. *21 Million People Are Now Victims of Forced Labour, ILO Says.* 1 June 2012. Web. 24 April 2013. <http://www.ilo.org/global/about-the-ilo/newsroom/news/WCMS_181961/lang--en/index.htm>.

2 "Slavery: A 21st Century Evil." 25 November 2011. Television. Web. 20 March 2013.<http://www.aljazeera.com/programmes/slaverya21stcenturyevil/>.

3 Ibid

animals from morning until night."[4] These horrors have been told of by Jamila, a former bride slave. She tells of how her traffickers kidnapped and drugged her, before selling her to an abusive man.

"He would hit me and beat me day and night. I would have to work all day in the heat .... That's no life .... Is it worth living?"[5]

---

[4] "Slavery: A 21st Century Evil." 25 November 2011. Television. Web. 20 March 2013.<http://www.aljazeera.com/programmes/slaverya21stcenturyevil/>.

[5] Ibid

MAYA LINSTRUM-NEWMAN

ARTICLE 5
THE PROHIBITION OF TORTURE IS ABSOLUTE, EXCEPT IN RELATION TO THOSE PESKY FOREIGNERS, OF COURSE

"No one shall be subjected to torture or to cruel, inhuman or degrading treatment or punishment."

Under international law, the prohibition on torture is absolute. It's absolute nature is outlined not only in Article 5 of the Universal Declaration of Human Rights, but also in other international human rights treaties as well as in regional and domestic instruments. More significantly, the prohibition has come to be considered a 'jus cogens' norm: a fundamental norm of international law, from which there can be no derogation. This absolute prohibition applies to all conduct outlined in Article 5, and to inhumane and degrading treatment and punishment, termed by some as 'torture lite'.[1]

Numerous legal scholars and moral philosophers have highlighted the importance of the absolute nature of this prohibition. David Sussman, for example, describes torture as a 'special type of wrong' in that it 'forces the victim to collude against themselves so that they are simultaneously powerless and yet at the same time complicit in their own violation… a kind of self-betrayal more akin to rape.'[2] Jeremy Waldron provides arguably the most convincing defence of the absolute nature of this prohibition, describing it's 'metastatic tendency', in that it 'has shown itself not to be the sort of thing that can be kept under rational control.'[3] More importantly, he asserts that '(these rights)…were designated long ago as absolutes precisely because of the temptation to rethink them or relativize them in times of panic, insecurity, and anger'.[4] Waldron also draws on Robert Nozick's argument[5] that torture makes the balance between liberty and security inter-personal rather than intra-personal and argues that using another person 'for the benefit of others does not take account of the fact that he is a separate person, that his life is the only life he has'.

Most significantly however, irrespective of the merit of any of his moral arguments for the absolute prohibition, Waldron asserts that absolute prohibition, in law, cannot be doubted: 'there is no balancing in Law in relation to torture'. He uses the case of Guantanamo Bay to illustrate this, asserting that 'protests against the use of such techniques in Guantanamo came much more consistently from military officials than clergymen or moral philosophers', thus suggesting a departure from what may be

---

[1] Campbell, Duncan. "US Interrogators Turn to 'Torture Lite'." 25 July 2003. Web. 12 April 2013. <http://www.guardian.co.uk/world/2003/jan/25/usa.alqaida>.

[2] Sussman, David. "What's Wrong With Torture?" *Philosophy and Public Affairs* 33.1 (2005): 1-33.

[3] Shue, Henry. "Torture." *Philosophy and Public Affairs* 7.2 (Winter, 1978): 124-143.

[4] Waldron, Jeremy. Introduction. *Torture, Terror and Trade-Offs: Philosophy for the White House*. Oxford: Oxford University Press, 2010.

[5] Nozick, Robert. *Anarchy, State, and Utopia*. Cornwall: Blackwell Publishing Limited, 2001, pp. 32–3.

traditionally seen as the predominantly moral basis for this absolute.

Therefore if Waldron is right and the legal prohibition under Article 5 is absolute, then it follows that it will of course then apply in every context, including cases of foreign nationals whom the state wishes to deport. Unsurprisingly, the case law of regional tribunals, such as the European Court of Human Rights, initially appears to support this.

Article 3 of the ECHR states that '(N)o one shall be subjected to torture or to inhuman or degrading treatment or punishment.' In the case *Soering v UK*[6], the extra-territorial effect of Article 3 of the ECHR was established, regarding the deportation of a foreign national, and thus exposure of them to ill-treatment outside of the jurisdiction of the Contracting States. It was therefore held that Soering could not be deported because his, 'extradition to the United States would expose him to a real risk of treatment going beyond the threshold set by Article 3 (art. 3)'.

The absolute prohibition of torture and inhuman and degrading treatment was even extended to extradition cases involving national security. In *Chahal v UK*[7], the European Court was of the opinion that 'it is not necessary for the Court to enter into consideration about the Government's allegations about the applicant's threat to national security' and this approach was reaffirmed in *Saadi v Italy*[8] where the Court held that the argument submitted by the UK as a third party intervener, based on the balancing of the risk of harm to the person against the risk they pose to the Community, was 'misconceived'. Therefore, perhaps we should have faith in Waldron's assertion that the legal prohibition of torture is still 'unequivocal and unconditional'.

And yet, it seems that the effect of the War on Terror, in practice, is to dilute the absolute nature of Article 5 in general, with the brunt of the dilution being felt by foreign nationals facing deportation and refoulement (refoulement being the expulsion of a person with the right to be recognised as a refugee to a country in which they will face persecution).[9] With legal scholars such as Dershowitz advocating a 'necessity doctrine',[10] it is perhaps unsurprising that this has filtered down into the judicial application of the prohibition against torture and it seems that in the case of extraditions, some balancing has been permitted by courts: firstly in terms of assessing whether the treatment in the receiving State will reach the *minimum level of severity* required to invoke the relevant treaty article, and secondly in terms of assessing *the risk* of a violation of that article by the

---

[6] *Soering v. The United Kingdom,* 1/1989/161/217, Council of Europe: European Court of Human Rights, 7 July 1989.

[7] *Chahal v. The United Kingdom*, 70/1995/576/662. Council of Europe: European Court of Human Rights, 15 November 1996.

[8] *Saadi v. Italy*, 37201/06, Council of Europe: European Court of Human Rights, 28 February 2008.

[9] "Non-refoulement." United Nations Educational, Scientific and Cultural Organization. Web. 16 April 2013. <http://www.unesco.org/new/en/social-and-human-sciences/themes/international-migration/glossary/refoulement/>.

[10] Dershowitz, Alan. "Tortured Reasoning," *International Human Rights in Context: Law, Politics, Morals*. Ed. Henry J. Steiner, Ryan Goodman and Philip Alston, 3rd ed. Oxford: Oxford University Press, 2008. 250.

receiving State.

In relation firstly to the effect of the dilution in the context of assessments as to whether the treatment will reach the minimum severity required to invoke the protection of the relevant treaty article, let us look to the case of *Babar Ahmad and others v UK*[11] in the European Court of Human Rights. Whilst it was reaffirmed that 'the prohibition provided by Article 3 against ill-treatment is equally absolute in expulsion cases' the judgement also established the contrary, that 'the absolute nature of Article 3 does not mean that any form of ill-treatment will act as a bar to removal from a Contracting State…treatment which might violate Article 3 because of an act or an omission of a contracting state might not attain the minimum level of severity which is required for there to be a violation of Article 3 in an expulsion or extradition case'.

Moreover, it is possible that the effect of the War on Terror is such that there has been a dilution of the absolute prohibition when assessing the minimum level of severity in all cases, not just in those involving elements of national security, as demonstrated by the case of *N v UK*[12]. Here, it was found that deporting an AIDS sufferer back to Uganda did not constitute a violation of Article 3 of the ECHR, despite the inhumane and degrading treatment she would suffer due to inadequate healthcare facilities in Uganda, as this could only be applied to the most 'exceptional circumstances' (as were in *D v UK*[13]). Whilst not affording an AIDS sufferer adequate healthcare in the UK would clearly constitute a violation of Article 3, the obligation was not extended extra-territorially in this case.

Therefore the minimum level of severity required to invoke the protection of the Convention is now much higher in relation to the ill-treatment a state exposes foreign nationals to abroad.

Secondly then, let us look to the dilution of protection in the context of the establishment of the actual risk of such ill-treatment. In order for the extra-territorial obligation of the deporting State to be engaged, the European Court has long held that there must be a real or substantial risk of torture or inhuman or degrading treatment or punishment. In assessing this risk, the Court has often relied on 'diplomatic assurances' from the receiving State in order to mitigate the risk.

In the case of *(Othman) Abu-Qatada v UK*[14], whilst the court dismissed that the applicant could not be deported to Jordan due to a real or substantial risk of a breach of his rights under Article 6 of the ECHR, the diplomatic assurance submitted by Jordan that he would not be tortured (Article 3) was in fact accepted by the Court.

Amnesty International has identified that 'the use of diplomatic assurances against

---

[11] *Babar Ahmad and others v. The United Kingdom*, 24027/07, Council of Europe: ECHR 609, 10 April 2012.

[12] *N. v. The United Kingdom*, 26565/05, Council of Europe: ECHR 453, 27 May 2008.

[13] *D. v. The United Kingdom*, 146/1996/767/964, Council of Europe: ECHR, 2 May 1997.

[14] *Othman (Abu Qatada) v. The United Kingdom*, 8139/09, Council of Europe: ECHR, 17 April 2012, 56.

torture has increased considerably following the 11 September 2001 attacks on the USA'[15] and their expert on human rights and counter-terrorism, Julia Hall has identified the problem of this, 'European governments must recommit to the fundamentals of human rights protection. That means safeguarding people from abuse by abiding by their international obligation. Diplomatic assurances do not provide such a safeguard and the practice of relying on this should be abandoned starting now'.[16]

A number of academics have also referred to the problems with diplomatic assurances. Lena Skoglund highlights how 'diplomatic assurances in order to protect against torture have been sought since the introduction of the obligation of non-refoulement to torture',[17] but the effect of the War on Terror has increased their use dramatically. The inability of diplomatic assurances to safeguard the absolute nature of the prohibition is due to, according to Skoglund, the fact that 'there exists no regulation regarding assurances against torture' as 'such assurances are not mentioned in international human rights treaties, and...thus, largely remain a 'grey area of international law'.

Therefore it seems clear that, in the European context, the prohibition of the ill treatment under Article 3 can no longer be regarded as absolute. However, the dilution of the absolute nature of the prohibition is not solely in relation to Article 3 of the European Convention on Human Rights, but has occurred in the context of all international human rights instruments.

Joseph, Schultz and Castan in their commentary on the application of the International Covenant of Civil and Political Rights[18] stated that apart from *C v Australia*[19], that concerned a very specific issue in which the applicant had already been granted refugee status due to his 'well-founded fear of persecution', the Human Rights Committee has found a violation of Article 7 entailed in a proposed deportation only on one occasion[20].

Moreover, we see that the same issue of establishing a 'real and substantial risk' applies in the international sphere. Even the CAT Committee when applying Article 3 of the Convention Against Torture, which specifically states that 'No State Party shall expel, return ("refouler") or extradite a person to another State where there are substantial grounds for believing that he would be in danger of being subjected to torture', stated in *Mutombo v Switzerland* that 'the existence of a consistent pattern of human rights

---

[15] "Europe Must Halt Unreliable 'Diplomatic Assurances' That Risk Torture." *Amnesty International.* 12 April 2010. Web. 15 April 2013. <http://www.amnesty.org/en/news-and-updates/report/europe-must-halt-unreliable-diplomatic-assurances-risk-torture-2010-04-12>.

[16] Ibid

[17] Skoglund, Lena. "Diplomatic Assurances Against Torture – An Effective Strategy?" *Nordic Journal of International Law* 77.4 (2008): 319-364.

[18] Joseph, Sarah, Jenny Schultz and Melissa Castan, *The International Covenant on Civil and Political Rights: Cases, Commentary and Materials*. Oxford: Oxford Univerysity Press, 2000.

[19] *C. v. Australia*, CCPR/C/76/D/900/1999, UN Human Rights Committe, 13 November 2002

[20] *Charles Chitat Ng v. Canada*, CCPR/C/49/D/469/1991, UN Human Rights Committee, 7 January 1994.

violations is not enough to prohibit extradition'.[21]

To conclude then, the prohibition outlined in Article 5 of the UDHR can no longer be regarded as absolute in relation to the deportation of foreign nationals, both in the regional context in the application of Article 3 of the European Convention on Human Rights, and in the international context in the application of Article 7 of the ICCPR and Article 3 of the Convention against Torture. This is due to both a narrowing of the treatment that will fall within the scope of the relevant Articles and an increasing of the amount of evidence that is required to demonstrate the real and substantial risk of such treatment. It seems that Theresa May's desire to 'put Qatada on a plane and get him out of our country for good'[22], irrespective of the torture he faces in Jordan, is consistent with the rhetoric of the international community as a whole and judgments such as *Soering v UK* must now be considered by those of us who expect more from human rights, as merely a thing of the past.

---

[21] *Balabou Mutombo v. Switzerland*, CAT/C/12/D/013/1993, UN Committe Against Torture, 27 April 1994.

[22] Judd, Terri. "Abu Qatada Stays in UK: Theresa May Under Pressure After Another Judicial Rebuff." *The Independent.* 27 March 2013. Web. 16 April 2013. <http://www.independent.co.uk/news/uk/home-news/abu-qatada-stays-in-uk-theresa-may-under-pressure-after-another-judicial-rebuff-8550895.html>.

RACHEL BLACKFORD

ARTICLE 6
THE FREE WORLD?

"Everyone has the right to recognition everywhere as a person before the law."

The United States of America portrays an image of itself internationally as the primary advocate and defender of human rights. However, does this image really match up to its actions? Article 6 of the Universal Declaration of Human Rights (UDHR) states that 'everyone has the right to recognition everywhere as a person before the law', but a few cases seem to show that the US does not always fully respect this Article, most notably in the recent killing of Osama Bin Laden, but also in the ongoing issue of Guantanamo Bay. If the 'leader of the free world' does not always uphold this Article, what is the outlook for human rights in the future?

On 2 May 2011, Osama bin Laden, the founder and head of the Islamist militant group Al-Qaeda, was killed in Pakistan by US Navy SEALs. The reaction to this news was mixed. In general, US public opinion seemed supportive of the action, and popular demonstrations to celebrate the news were widespread in major cities across the country.[1] Many key US political figures also welcomed and celebrated the news, for example calling it a 'victory for America'[2] (George W. Bush), and both NATO and the EU claimed it had increased international security.[3] However, not all responses to the news were so positive. Pakistan rebuked the US for its covert, unilateral action on its soil, and the Muslim Brotherhood in Egypt called the killing of Bin Laden an 'assassination'.[4] Human rights groups such as Amnesty International have questioned the killing of Osama Bin Laden, and why attempts were not made to capture him alive.[5] While his crimes against humanity are undoubtedly serious and should clearly be condemned, the issue of the US's compliance with international human rights law, such as Article 6 of the UDHR, is fundamental.

Article 6 of the UDHR states that 'everyone has the right to recognition everywhere as a person before the law', which seems to clearly mean that whatever a person's crimes, they have the right to a fair trial in a court. The US's killing of Bin Laden without attempting to capture him alive to bring him to trial in court seems to directly challenge this principle. Despite the magnitude of the allegations against Bin Laden and his crimes against humanity, the US, as purportedly one of the key advocates of human rights worldwide, should have respected the UDHR and captured him alive, treating him as a

---

1 "Osama Bin Laden Killed: Worldwide Reactions." *The Atlantic: In Focus.* 2 May 2011. Web. 10 April 2013. <http://www.theatlantic.com/infocus/2011/05/osama-bin-laden-killed-worldwide-reactions/100058/>.

2 "Osama Bin Laden's Death: Political Reaction in Quotes." *BBC News: US and Canada.* 3 May 2011. Web. 10 April 2013. <http://www.bbc.co.uk/news/world-us-canada-13256956>.

3 CNN Wire Staff. "World Leaders React to News of Bin Laden's Death." *CNN.* 3 May 2011. Web. 10 April 2013. <http://edition.cnn.com/2011/WORLD/asiapcf/05/02/bin.laden.world.reacts/index.html>.

4 Chulov, Martin. "Egypt's Muslim Brotherhood Says Bin Laden Should Have Been Tried." *The Guardian.* 2 May 2011. Web. 10 April 2013. <http://www.guardian.co.uk/world/2011/may/02/egypt-muslim-brotherhood-bin-laden-tried>.

5 "Osama Bin Laden: More Information Needed on Circumstances of Killing." *Amnesty International.* 4 May 2011. Web. 10 April 2013. <http://www.amnesty.org.uk/news_details.asp?NewsID=19439>.

person before the law. Giving Bin Laden a fair trial in court would have been a much stronger demonstration of the value of human rights and a much stronger statement against terrorism than the course of action the US chose.

The US defended the killing rather than capture of Bin Laden by appealing to a resolution passed by Congress after the attacks of 11 September 2001: the 'Authorisation for Use of Military Force Against Terrorists' allowed the President to use 'necessary and appropriate force against those nations, organisations, or persons' he determined were involved in the attacks.[6] The threat of terrorism has been used on several occasions in recent years to justify infringements on human rights laid out in the UDHR,[7] and the case of Bin Laden shows very clearly how the threat of terrorism was used to justify violating Article 6 of the UDHR. However, surely human rights should be applied without exception, whatever the case; if we start choosing when to apply certain Articles of the UDHR and when to ignore them, then the value of these Articles is lost, and the norms of human rights are weakened. The US identifies itself as a leader of the human rights movement worldwide,[8] so surely it should set an example in this, rather than use its great power status to choose to ignore certain Articles when it suits the country's interests. If Article 6 is to be a truly universally respected principle by all sovereign nations, there should be no exceptions to its application, whatever crimes the subject has committed. While the US made claims that capturing Bin Laden would have been logistically impossible, accounts of him being armed are mixed,[9] so it may not be that the Navy SEALs had to kill him in an act of self-defence.

The issue of Guantanamo Bay also casts doubt on the US's upholding of Article 6 of the UHDR. Here, allegations of torture persist,[10] as well as issues of holding detainees without access to a fair trial;[11] both these allegations again show how the US may not be treating everyone as a 'person before the law', and setting an example that respecting human rights is situationally dependent.

The US cannot uphold its image of being one of the main worldwide human rights advocates while these abuses of one of the most basic principles continues. The very essence of the Universal Declaration, and indeed Article 6, is these norms should not be violated under any circumstances, not even those relating to terrorism, especially by a great power that should be setting a strong example for other states to follow. If the US is serious about wanting to spread human rights norms across the globe, it must start by

---

[6] Bellinger III, John B. "A Counterterrorism Law in Need of Updating." *The Washington Post.* 26 November 2010. Web. 10 April 2013. <http://www.washingtonpost.com/wp-dyn/content/article/2010/11/25/AR2010112503116.html>.

[7] Ibid

[8] Barnett, Michael. "Is America the Moral Leader in the World?" *CNN.* 4 July 2012. Web. 10 April 2013. <http://edition.cnn.com/2012/07/04/opinion/barnett-human-rights>.

[9] "Osama Bin Laden: More Information Needed on Circumstances of Killing." *Amnesty International.* 4 May 2011. Web. 10 April 2013. <http://www.amnesty.org.uk/news_details.asp?NewsID=19439>.

[10] "Guantanamo: In His Second Term Obama Must Correct Human Rights Failure." *Amnesty International.* 8 January 2013. Web. 10 April 2013. <https://www.amnesty.org/en/news/guant-namo-his-second-term-obama-must-correct-human-rights-failure-2013-01-08>.

[11] Ibid

setting an example for others to follow. Even though its great power status means the US can 'get away with' violating Articles of the UDHR without being greatly challenged, the negative effect these violations have on the norms of human rights are still hugely significant. If the US is to continue choosing when to obey and when to disobey certain Articles, such as Article 6, when it suits their interests, then the status of human rights on a global scale could be irrevocably damaged.

Jamie Pelling

Article 7
The Bangladeshi War Crimes Tribunal

"All are equal before the law and are entitled without any discrimination to equal protection of the law. All are entitled to equal protection against any discrimination in violation of this Declaration and against any incitement to such discrimination."

Towards the end of Lent Term, the LSESU Amnesty International Society invited Mr Toby Cadman to speak about the Bangladeshi War Crimes Tribunal. Mr Cadman works for the defence, he is defending people accused of the most horrible crimes imaginable, hardly the most likely guest of a society which aims to raise awareness of Human Rights abuse on campus and condemn it in all its forms. More surprisingly, Mr Cadman is an international criminal lawyer who has worked on numerous Human Rights cases; he helped the prosecution in the Bosnian War Crimes Tribunals and has worked with the Syrian opposition. It was in that role that he was first invited to speak for the LSESU Amnesty International Society. Evidently, there is more to this picture than a known defender of Human Rights choosing to abandon his principles and attempt to protect war criminals. The missing link in the puzzle is strongly linked to Article 7. Mr Cadman believes that judicial process has been abandoned in this Tribunal, preventing a fair trial from taking place.

Without wishing to bypass the legal arguments outlined by Mr Cadman in his lecture, more detail may be found online, it seems clear that when Ambassador Rapp visited Bangladesh under the auspices of the UN he made some recommendations to ensure the fairness of the tribunal. Mr Cadman posits that these recommendations have not been implemented and, indeed, Ambassador Rapp has consented to return and assess this implementation. It is important that Bangladesh solves this problem by itself, but there is a role for the international community in assisting, with financial, intellectual, or legal aid. Bangladesh has not received any of this, unlike the Bosnian Tribunal. It has also not been part of any Western media spotlight, again unlike Bosnia. It is ignored by the international community at a time when support is desperately needed. This may all seem to be academic. Mr Cadman did not go into evidential detail concerning the case, but it seems probable that many of the men on trial are guilty. Why then, as one audience member demanded of Mr Cadman, should there be such a concern over their legal protection? Because equality of protection before the law is at the heart of judicial fairness, and at the heart of Human Rights. Whoever is on trial, be it a sixteen year old boy who hijacked a car, a fraudulent banker, or a war criminal in Bangladesh, deserves the same right to equality before the law, and it is for this reason that Amnesty International, Human Rights Watch, and the UN are keeping such a close eye on this Tribunal.

NATALIE SYKES

ARTICLE 8
THE UK HUMAN RIGHTS ACT: INHERENTLY UNDEMOCRATIC OR A NECESSARY PROTECTION OF HUMAN RIGHTS IN THE UK?

"Everyone has the right to an effective remedy by the competent national tribunals for acts violating the fundamental rights granted him by the constitution or by law."

There is an ongoing debate surrounding the democratic applicability of bills of rights: some echo Thomas Jefferson's statement that bills of rights are "what the people are entitled to against every government on earth" while others claim that, given the necessity of their interpretation, bills of rights are inherently undemocratic. Indeed, it seems bills of rights may at once protect the population from undue power of the executive branch of government by providing for legally entrenched rights, while having the potential to limit a democratically elected government's ability to carry out necessary reforms in areas where there is no settled human rights answer.[1] Bills of rights address contentious human rights questions that evolve as society changes – questions surrounding the right to life and the right to privacy – which means that their formulation is necessarily open ended. Therefore, bills of rights require interpretation, which opens the door to manipulation on the part of legislatures and courts.

This task of interpretation falls to the courts – and, as a result, the judges who make up these courts. Perhaps the heart of the argument underpinning a view of bills of rights as inherently undemocratic is the range of grey areas inherent in most, if not all, articulations of rights in such documents. Just looking at the case of abortion and the right to life makes this abundantly clear; for a judge with conservative values, the right to life rightly includes a foetus and therefore abortion violates the right to life. On the other side of the spectrum, a judge who subscribes to a more scientifically informed view of life may see an acceptable window during which abortion is acceptable. Given that so many human rights issues are inherently political, and comprise so many grey areas, bills of rights are seen as undemocratic in that they transfer the final say on these contentious issues to the judicial arena. For some, this amounts to subverting democratic discourse.

For example, the European Convention on Human Rights (which the UK Human Rights Act effectively imports into UK law as a UK Bill of Rights) contains limitations to all rights save for the freedom of conscience, freedom from torture and from slavery. The interpretation of the limitations to rights is only guided by the statements that such limitations must be 'prescribed by law' and be 'necessary in a democratic society.' What exactly is necessary in a democratic society is up to the interpretation of Parliament, with courts merely able to issue declarations of incompatibility if legislation passed is perceived as violating a convention right beyond what is deemed, in their eyes, to be necessary.

However, many strongly argue that bills of rights – and the UK Human Rights Act – are necessary to protect minorities from the majoritarian impulses of democratically elected governments. As Gearty and Ewing argue in a 1996 pamphlet produced for the Society of Labour Lawyers, the principle of judicial review is not incompatible with

[1] Klug, Francesca. "A Bill of Rights: What For?" *Towards a New Constitutional Settlement,* Ed. Chris Bryant MP, The Smith Institute, 2007.

democracy as it is necessary to protect against 'democratically elected despots.' As Lord Irvine eloquently stated, the UK Human Rights Act delivers 'a modern reconciliation of the inevitable tension between the democratic right of the majority to exercise political power and the democratic need of individuals and minorities to have their human rights secured.'[2]As Francesca Klug writes, bills of rights 'not only protect the rights of individuals but can have a symbolic role in highlighting the fundamental principles of a democracy…bills of rights can act as a baseline of common values in a diverse society.'[3] In this sense, the UK Human Rights Act is an important piece of legislation that at once enforces the values articulated in article 8 of the Universal Declaration while affirming a basic commitment to the protection of human rights in the UK.

---

[2] Irvine, Derry (Lord Irvine of Lairg QC), "The Human Rights Act: Principle and Practice." *Parliamentary Affairs* 57.4 (2004): 744-753.

[3] Klug, Francesca. "A Bill of Rights: what for?" *Towards a New Constitutional Settlement,* Ed. Chris Bryant MP, The Smith Institute, 2007.

JASIM MALIK

ARTICLES 9 AND 10
BRITISH HUMAN RIGHTS: ARE OUR COURTS IMPARTIAL?

Article 9: "No one shall be subjected to arbitrary arrest, detention or exile."

Article 10: "Everyone is entitled in full equality to a fair and public hearing by an independent and impartial tribunal, in the determination of his rights and obligations and of any criminal charge against him."

British human rights have their origins in the English Bill of Rights in 1689. In the modern post-war world Britain has consistently put herself at the forefront of the glorified global call for freedom and equality for all, being a signatory of the 1949 Geneva Rights Convention and since then a participant of comprehensive pan-European legislation standardizing the concepts of equality of citizen protection in each respective nation.

However, whilst Britain has often been a self-proclaimed leader in the push for greater respect for human rights across the world, the UK also has a dogmatic history of persistent institutional discrimination. Whilst the issues that once prevented the emergence of a socially cohesive multicultural society have since faded into the background, worrying trends in the selective application of British justice for British citizens have emerged. This article will explore whether Britain has been fulfilling Articles 9 and 10 of the Universal Declaration of Human Rights.

Since the seismic events of 9/11, the abuse of civil liberties in Britain has become an accepted and rarely discussed reality of today's society. Whilst most Britons are unaffected by certain sweeping legislations passed since 2001[1], these developments have had appalling effects on certain minorities that are as entitled to be protected by the law as any other. Figures published by the Home Office in May 2009 revealed that two-thirds of those arrested for terrorism in Britain since 9/11 have later been released without charge.[2] The figures show that 1,471 people were arrested on suspicion of terrorism between 11 September 2001 and 31 March last year, but only 340 were charged with terrorism-related offences. So far, the courts have convicted only 196 of those charged with such offences.[3]

I'm British; Extradite Me!

The most prominent example of this is the recent controversial extradition of 5 'terror suspects' to the United States, where they can be held indefinitely in solitary confinement with no trial for any given amount of time.[4] The media played an unhelpful role by skewing the issue in continuously

[1] United Kingdom. *Criminal Justice Act 2003.* s225. Web. 7 January 2013.<http://www.legislation.gov.uk/ukpga/2003/44/section/225>.

[2] Travis, Alan. "Two-Thirds of UK Terror Suspects Released Without Charge." *The Guardian.* 13 May 2009. Web. 17 April 2013. <http://www.guardian.co.uk/uk/2009/may/13/terrorism-suspects-britain-uk>.

[3] Ibid

[4] Casciani, Dominic. "The Battle to Prosecute Babar Ahmad." *BBC News: UK.* 5 April 2012. Web. 17 April 2013. <http://www.bbc.co.uk/news/uk-17606337>.

referring to the suspects as "Abu Humza and 4 others"[5], tarring the other suspects as if their respective cases as are well evidenced and their guilt as confirmed as that of Abu Humza: unlike the other suspects, Abu Humza has been put on trial and found guilty in the U K .

However, this was clearly not the case with both Babar Ahmad and Talha Ahsan. Babar Ahmad was held for more than 7 years in prison without trial, and his recent extradition was concluded despite the fact that the evidence against him had not been presented to British courts, nor had it been put under any independent scrutiny.[6] And whilst the thought that a British citizen can remain in jail for years on end without trial is tremendously worrying[7], the case of Talha Ahsan is even more troubling given the parallels in the case with that of Gary McKinnon – and the contrasting outcomes of their respective extradition processes. Both Talha Ahsan and Gary McKinnon are wanted by the US for allegedly committing crimes online, and both could face lengthy prison sentences of 60 years and beyond. However, Home Secretary Theresa May intervened in the case of McKinnon and in a statement claimed that "(A) decision to extradite would be incompatible with [Mr McKinnon's] human rights."[8] This was because McKinnon suffered from Asperger's Syndrome – a medical condition that required him to stay in the UK to avoid any potential suffering he may experience as a result of facing American prison.

On the face of it, this decision makes sense. However, one glaring contradiction comes to mind; Talha Ahsan, extradited 2 weeks before this decision, also has Asperger's Syndrome. Does Talha not have the same human rights as Gary McKinnon; is it not true his rights would have been infringed if he was extradited given his similar medical afflictions? Apparently not, according to Theresa May[9]. This highlights what may inevitably be seen by many, particularly Muslim minorities living in the UK, as a hypocritical stand on human rights that is invalid where Muslim terror suspects are concerned.

The powerful argument that the crimes Babar Ahmad and Talha Ahsan are alleged to have committed were within the UK jurisdiction, and thus they should be tried in British

---

[5] Harris, Paul. "Abu Hamza and Four Other Suspects Appear in US Courts After Extradition." *The Guardian.* 6 October 2012. Web. 7 January 2013. <http://www.guardian.co.uk/world/2012/oct/06/abu-hamza-us-court-extradition1>.
"Abu Hamza Among Five Terror Suspects Extradited to US." *BBC News: UK.* 6 October 2012. Web. 7 January 2013. <http://www.bbc.co.uk/news/uk-19853903>.
Holehouse, Matthew. "Extradition of Abu Hamza and Four Others for Terrorism Offences Can Go Ahead European Court Rules." *The Telegraph.* 10 April 2012. Web. 7 January 2013. <http://www.telegraph.co.uk/news/uknews/terrorism-in-the-uk/9195024/Extradition-of-Abu-Hamza-and-four-others-for-terrorism-offences-can-go-ahead-European-court-rules.html>.

[6] Casciani, Dominic. "Babar Ahmad Appeals For Trial to be Held in UK." *BBC News: UK.* 5 April 2012. Web. 17 April 2013. <http://www.bbc.co.uk/news/uk-17614935>.

[7] Holcroft-Emmess, Natasha. "James, Wells and Lee v UK: Indefinite Detention and Arbitrary Deprivations of Liberty." *Oxford Human Rights Hub.* 27 November 2012. Web. 7 January 2013. <http://ohrh.law.ox.ac.uk/?p=710>.

[8] "Gary McKinnon Extradition to US Blocked by Theresa May." *BBC News: UK.* 16 October 2012. Web. 7 January 2013. <http://www.bbc.co.uk/news/uk-19957138>.

[9] Ibid

courts, is another argument entirely that warrants its own investigation. However, even more recently a perhaps more appalling case has come to light.

British Citizenship; No Guarantee

Arguably the most worrying case of human rights abuses tacitly being approved by the UK government is that of Mahdi Hashi. You'd be forgiven if you hadn't heard of the name; despite the extraordinary nature of his story as an ex-British citizen, it hasn't received the warranted media attention.

Mahdi Hashi had grown up in North London, but from the age of 16 onwards was subject to 'harassment' by the MI5[10], which involved being detained at UK airports and seemingly random deportations, allegedly at the request of the British government. Eventually Mahdi was asked to become an informant for the intelligence agency, and after being bombarded with phone calls he eventually sought to escape the pressure by return to his native Somalia to care for his ill grandmother, where he later married.

Three years after his leaving Britain he disappeared without a trace, and his whereabouts only became known when an inmate of an American prison in Djibouti was released who claimed to have been with young Mahdi.[11] It was at this time that the British government announced that it was revoking Mahdi's citizenship for his involvement in 'terrorist activities', and was now deemed a threat to Britain's national security. Upon being questioned as to why the decision had been made, the Home Office refused to give further details and instead claimed that the move had been made based on 'secret evidence' that could not be disclosed due to its implications on national security[12]; a dubious claim at best.

This threatens to set a precedent for the revoking of citizenship for anyone arbitrarily deemed 'involved in terrorist activities', and there is a mounting case that indicates the British government's anti-terror zeal has significantly eroded civil liberties in clear contravention of the 9th and 10th Articles of the Universal Declaration of Human Rights. That the aforementioned cases have received less media attention that the importance of what is at stake should warrant, and that media coverage has tended to put the government's extra-judicial decisions under less scrutiny than is needed, highlights a dangerous trend that involves systematic inconsistencies in application of British law, which may breed increasing resentment amongst communities in the country.

[10] "The Betrayal of Mahdi Hashi." *CagePrisoners.* 2 November 2012. Web. 7 January 2013. <http://www.cageprisoners.com/our-work/opinion-editorial/item/5276-the-betrayal-of-mahdi-hashi>.

[11] Kermani, Secunder. "Mahdi Hashi has British Citizenship Revoked for Extremism." *BBC News: London.* 1 November 2012. Web. 7 January 2013.<http://www.bbc.co.uk/news/uk-england-london-20157167>.

[12] "Mahdi Hashi has British Citizenship Revoked for Extremism." *BBC News: London.* 3 November 2012. Web. 7 January 2013 <http://www.bbc.co.uk/news/uk-england-london-20191899>.

Elizabeth Stout

Article 11
A Questionable Doctrine

"(1) Everyone charged with a penal offence has the right to be presumed innocent until proved guilty according to law in a public trial at which he has had all the guarantees necessary for his defence.
(2) No one shall be held guilty of any penal offence on account of any act or omission which did not constitute a penal offence, under national or international law, at the time when it was committed. Nor shall a heavier penalty be imposed than the one that was applicable at the time the penal offence was committed."

It has become a truth almost universally acknowledged that national security cannot be compromised for the sake of human rights. Such a compromise was not made by the United Nations Security Council in imposing Resolution 1267 against a Mr Kadi in 2001.[1] Resolution 1267 allowed that, in response to an increase in terrorism in the Afghan region, those who were seen to be involved with al-Qaeda or the Taliban were to have all funds and financial assets frozen. Yet while such requirements are no doubt in breach of many Articles of the UDHR, the Resolution went further. It provided that such suspects were to have their names placed on a 'blacklist', along with any other individual under suspicion of involvement with terrorist activity. This blacklist would be accessible to states, who were under obligations to enforce the above sanctions against any on the list. Those listed upon it, however, would not be aware of this. Herein lies the violation of Article 11(1) of the Universal Declaration. The UN Security Council did not allow Mr Kadi a trial before placing him on the list, nor did they therefore adhere to the requirement of 'innocent until proved guilty.'

It must be noted, however, that the UDHR is not binding upon member states to the UN, nor indeed upon any state. It is merely a Declaration made by the UN General Assembly. While these rights are thus in principle agreed to by a majority of nations, this need not be the case in practice. Thus Mr Kadi could not object to his position on the list as a result of its violations of his rights under the Universal Declaration. However, binding law on human rights fortunately does exist; in this case the European Convention on Human Rights created a legally binding obligation upon EU States to respect Mr Kadi's rights. Thus, once the asset freeze and listing were carried out by the European Union, Mr Kadi could, and did, protest at the violations of his rights, under Articles 1 and 6 of the ECHR.[2] Article 6 of the ECHR is the right to due process, including the rights to trial as outlined in Article 11 of the UDHR.

In this case, the European Court of Justice decided to overturn the application of Resolution 1267 in the EU territory.[3] This decision is therefore hailed as promoting and

---

[1] *Yassin Abdullah Kadi and Al Barakaat International Foundation v Council of the European Union and Commission of the European Communities*. European Court of Justice, 3 September 2008.

[2] De Burca, Grainne. "The European Court of Justice and the International Legal Order After *Kadi*" *Harvard International Law Journal* 51.1 (2010): 1-50 <http://www.harvardilj.org/articles/1-50.pdf>.

[3] Ibid.

even protecting Human Rights above national security.[4] In the post-9/11 world, it is often perceived that anything may be sacrificed in order to protect against the threat of terrorism. In ruling to overturn previous EU legislation, the ECJ took a decision in contravention to many Western views on security, most specifically those advocated by the Security Council.[5] That the ECJ deemed Mr. Kadi's rights to take primacy over both national security concerns and indeed what may be seen to be the traditional hierarchy of international law suggests a recognition of the inviolability of these rights.[6] Such an achievement must be noted as one crucial to the achievement of Article 11 of the Universal Declaration, in setting a precedent that decisions taken by the United Nations Security Council need not be inviolable if they allow for the violation of human rights.

It is important that the decision be regarded as an achievement. The work of organisations such as Amnesty International in bringing human rights and their frequent violations to the attention of governments, the media and the public may be seen to have created an environment in which legislating against right to trial and due process is unacceptable. However, while such an achievement is not to be diminished, Article 11 continues to be as vulnerable as any Article in the Universal Declaration. The decision of the ECJ in the *Kadi* case was subject to a great amount of criticism from many directions.[7] Among these critics were those wishing to maintain the primacy of international law and those fearing for national security.[8] This criticism suggested that perhaps an environment in which human rights norms could not be sacrificed was perhaps not such a welcome environment after all. The unique nature of the EU, in being a supranational body and a regional organisation for member states, does not readily enable a precedent to be set for other states or organisations to follow suit. Indeed, the attribution of the decision to the fact that the EU is seen as a 'sui generis',[9] or a unique case, suggests that the decision may not have influenced the future relationship between national security and human rights to any great extent.

We must find, however, that such a relationship should not be dependent on the nature of a particular institution. It is here that the protection of Article 11 once again becomes visibly vulnerable. If it is to be protected only by particular institutions, i.e. those with sufficient power and, arguably, support to do so, then the Universal Declaration may

---

[4] De Burca, Grainne. "The European Court of Justice and the International Legal Order After *Kadi*" *Harvard International Law Journal* 51.1 (2010): 1-50 <http://www.harvardilj.org/articles/1-50.pdf>.

[5] Ibid.

[6] Wessel, Ramses A. "The Kadi Case: Towards a More Substantive Hierarchy in International Law?" *International Organizations Law Review* 5.2 (2008): 323-327 <http://docserver.ingentaconnect.com.gate2.library.lse.ac.uk/deliver/connect/mnp/15723739/v5n2/s4.pdf?expires=1363542333&id=73364510&titleid=11567&accname=London+School+of+Economics&checksum=EEDC7F406A4874DA3BE939E3387F86B8>.

[7] Kokott, Juliane and Christoph Sobotta. "The Kadi Case - Constitutional Core Values and International Law - Finding the Balance?" *European Journal of International Law,* 23.4. (2012): 1015-1024 <http://ejil.oxfordjournals.org.gate2.library.lse.ac.uk/content/23/4/1015.full.pdf+html> .

[8] De Burca, Grainne. "The European Court of Justice and the International Legal Order After *Kadi*" *Harvard International Law Journal* 51.1 (2010): 1-50 <http://www.harvardilj.org/articles/1-50.pdf>.

[9] Drzemczewski, Andrew. "The Sui Generis Nature of the European Convention on Human Rights" *The International and Comparative Law Quarterly* 29.1 (1980): 54-63 <http://www.jstor.org.gate2.library.lse.ac.uk/stable/758752>.

not be 'universal.' Whilst we do note that Mr. Kadi was protected under EU law despite not being a citizen of the EU, we also note that his rights were only allowed for within the jurisdiction of the EU.

There is therefore much work to be done on the relationship between human rights and national security. This work cannot simply be targeted at the United Nations Security Council, international regional organisations and governments. What must be dealt with first and foremost are the attitudes held towards both national security and human rights that have developed in tandem arguably since the attacks of 11 September 2001. It is often perceived as an undermining of these catastrophic events to reassess the position on national security that developed in their wake. It may also be seen as a balance between vital freedoms; between the freedom from terror, and the freedom to possess the rights set out for us in the UDHR. It appears that the prevailing view is pessimistic, that one must be sacrificed for the sake of the other. And rights to a fair trial, to property and to many other things have been sacrificed for the right to life. But no such doctrine should be so readily accepted. To leave it unchallenged may lead to a further sacrifice of human rights for the sake of security. It must be acknowledged that in stating no priority of rights the Universal Declaration teaches us that the right to life may not hold priority above all other rights. If we are to allow violations such as freezing funds and movement, torture, and no right to trial, then perhaps we diminish that 'life' we hold a right to.

The *Kadi* case may have raised new questions regarding the relationship between human rights and security. This relationship must now be subject to continuous scrutiny.

JOHN BENSON

ARTICLE 12
THE LIMITATIONS OF ARTICLE 12

> *"No one shall be subjected to arbitrary interference with his privacy, family, home or correspondence, nor to attacks upon his honour and reputation. Everyone has the right to the protection of the law against such interference or attacks."*

Article 12 is enshrined in UK defamation laws. These state that Party A cannot make claims about Party B if the claims cause the reasonable person to lower their opinion of Party B.

There are three total defences to defamation. The first defence is *justification*, meaning the claims made are true. The second defence available is *fair comment*, meaning the claims made could have been genuinely believed by the reasonable person. The third and final defence available is *privilege*, meaning the claims were made in an exceptional environment (such as Parliament or a court of law). The burden of proof lies with the defendant, who must prove the claim can be justified with one of the three above defences.

The protection ensured by Article 12 has caused major issues within Britain. One of the most salient concerns is its protection of suspected criminals. The recent scandal involving Jimmy Savile illustrates this. Savile was heavily suspected of committing numerous incidents of child abuse and sexual offences between 1955 and 2009, yet allegations of this only emerged after his death in 2011. However, it was supposedly common knowledge amongst groups in the media that Savile had a reputation for abusing young girls. Roy Greenslade, writing in The Guardian, highlights just how close Paul Connew (Editor of the Sunday Mirror) came to publishing the allegations in 1994:

> "[Connew had] "credible and convincing" evidence from two women who claimed Savile had been guilty of abusing them at a children's home.
>
> Though "totally and utterly convinced" they were telling the truth, the paper's lawyers, after a careful assessment, decided it wasn't strong enough to risk publication… I am sure the same situation occurred elsewhere."[1] (The Guardian, 2012)

Thus Savile's alleged activity was allowed to continue for another 15 years, under the protection of Article 12.

Another issue with Article 12, is its unequal application within the UK. Different individuals have different access to economic and social capital; those with more capital are more able to access resources enforcing Article 12. Take, for example, the concept of the 'super-injunction'.[2] These are legally binding restrictions on publishing certain items.

---

[1] Greenslade, Roy "Jimmy Savile: Why the tabloids were unable to publish and be damned." *The Guardian.* 10 October 2012. Web. 13 March 2013. <http://www.guardian.co.uk/media/greenslade/2012/oct/10/jimmy-savile-bbc>.

[2] Cascani, Dominic. "Q&A: Super-injunctions." *BBC News: UK.* 20 May 2011. Web. 17 April 2013. <http://www.bbc.co.uk/news/uk-13473070>.

They also prevent the publishing of the very fact they exist. Ryan Giggs famously obtained a super-injunction to hide his extra-marital affair with Imogen Thomas. There was therefore no interference with his private life. However, it must be questioned whether this protection would be available to someone who possessed less economic and social capital. It is likely that the everyday person would be unlikely to obtain a super-injunction regarding their private life, due to the high legal costs and having a lower public profile, negating the need for such injunctions. Yet, Article 12, and the Convention in general, suggest(s) the law should apply equally to all. It therefore appears that Article 12 does not apply equally to all in the UK.

Although there are clear benefits to Article 12 of the Universal Declaration, there are numerous underlying issues with its application. It has been highlighted how it may protect serious criminals and assist in hiding their crimes, and how its application favours those rich in economic and social capital. However, these reflect a wider controversy with human rights in general – they apply to all. While Article 12 may protect criminals, it also protects those who could perhaps unnecessarily be affected by interference with their private life and attacks on their reputation. It is in noting the innocent people that it does protect, as well as highlighting its limitations, that we can begin to see how we may improve Article 12.

IRA LORANDOU

ARTICLE 13
THE UNDERRATED ARTICLE 13

"(1) Everyone has the right to freedom of movement and residence within the borders of each state (2) Everyone has the right to leave any country, including his own, and to return to his country."

Article 13 is probably one of the most underrated articles of the great Universal Declaration of Human Rights (UDHR). This article articulates the fundamental freedom of mobility, a freedom that is essential to the materialization of the other more popular articles in the UNDHR, as free movement can facilitate equality.

The article addresses "everyone", stating that "everyone has the right". These words point to the three interlocking qualities of human rights: "rights are natural, equal and universal"[1]. Through the assertive tone of these first few words it establishes the rights as self-evident, with no explanation as to why 'everyone has the right to the freedom of movement'. Self-evidence has been characteristic of human rights discourse from its very origins in the eighteenth century (and arguably even earlier than that). Here lies a paradox of the self-evidence claim of human rights discourse, if rights are so evident then why must we declare it? Lynn Hunt argues that the claim of human rights as self-evidence is based in its emotional appeal as well as its basis in 'reason', in the manner in which it "strikes a chord"[2]. For instance, in the case of Article 13, there is a great deal of empathy felt in the association of the freedom of movement and refugees who require the freedom to move to another place to ensure their security.

The word 'everyone' simultaneously universalizes and equalizes its addressee; if rights apply to everyone, worldwide, then everyone is effectively equal. Thus the law equates 'everyone' with human beings "as creature[s] capable of bearing its rights"[3], thus imagining a "particular kind of human activated as a legal and moral unit with rights that are formulated in a society"[4], all human beings equal in a society.

In this particular case, the law is prescribing the right to freedom of movement: the freedom both to leave one's country and to return. Unlike many of the other articles of the UDHR,[5] this particular article has little precedent. Although it was upheld in human rights declarations that would follow it (namely the European Convention on Human Rights), this right to freedom of movement is hardly mentioned in previous documents on human rights. The right to leave a nation was mentioned in the Magna Carta of 1215, "which stated that

---

[1] Hunt, Lynn. "Introduction." *Inventing Human Rights: A History.* New York: W.W. Norton, 2007.

[2] Ibid, p26

[3] Slaughter, Joseph. *Human Rights, Inc.: The World Novel, Narrative Form, and International Law.* New York: Fordham University Press, 2007.

[4] Ibid

[5] Such as Article 1: "all human beings are born free and equal in dignity and rights" which is an echo of previous human rights declarations, for example point one: "men are born and remain free and equal in rights", in the Declaration of the Rights of Man and Citizen. <http://www.hrcr.org/docs/frenchdec.html> Web. 29 March 2012.

everyone had the right to leave England, subject to feudal obligations"[6], and the French Constitution of 1791 proclaimed the right to leave a nation.[7] However, this right was absent from the two key declarations of human rights: the United States Declaration of Independence and the Declaration of the Rights of Man and of the Citizen. Moreover, even these few human rights documents that preceded the UDHR do not specify the right to *return* to one's own country.

Why, then, would the drafters in 1948 feel the need to specify that if one walks out the door of a nation state, that door would not shut behind them?

Freedom and movement have always been closely related. Yi-Fu Tuan argues that "freedom implies space, it means having the power and enough room in which to act"[8]. Mobility was explicitly promoted by the nation-states of Western Europe after the Second World War as they sought "to promote international understanding among the younger generation as a means of postwar reconciliation"[9]. Thus, the right to leave and return to one's nation was seen to promote a universalism which could traverse borders, a universalism which was essential in a post-war Europe which had seen the very worst effects of nationalism.

Yet, in practice, an open border cosmopolitanism does not exist in today's world order, which is still dominated by concepts of 'residence'[10], 'borders'[11] and a citizen's limit to 'his own country'[12]. Lynn Hunt claims that "human rights only become meaningful when they gain political content"[13]. In the broader discourse of human rights it has been the first few articles that have been afforded the most attention, especially Article One, 'all human beings are born free and equal in dignity and rights' and Article Three 'everyone has the right to life, liberty and security of person', with Article Thirteen being lost and forgotten. However the issue is, how can an individual have any of these rights without something as basic as the freedom to move? The 'right to life, liberty and security of person' remain abstract concepts without a concrete space in which the subject can claim them. With this in mind there are geographical limitations to claiming rights. In the current world order, excluding Europe's Schengen Agreement, it is still an endeavor to cross borders, especially if one lacks the finances. There are staunch immigration laws that have a profound effect upon other basic human rights, preventing mobility and forcing an individual to remain in a state that persecutes them for religion, sexuality, sex and so on.

---

[6] Weissbrodt, David S., and Connie De La. Vega. *International Human Rights Law: An Introduction.* Philadelphia: University of Pennsylvania, 2007. p71.

[7] Ibid

[8] Tuan, Yi-fu. *Space and Place: The Perspective of Experience.* Minneapolis: University of Minnesota, 1977. p52.

[9] Jobs, Richard Ivan. "Youth Movements: Travel, Protest, and Europe in 1968." *The American Historical Review* 114.2 (2009): 376-404.

[10] The United Nations Universal Declaration of Rights. Web. 24 April 2013. <http://www.un.org/en/documents/udhr/>.

[11] Ibid

[12] Ibid

[13] Hunt, Lynn. "Introduction." *Inventing Human Rights: A History.* New York: W.W. Norton, 2007, p21.

By preventing an individual's mobility, human rights can be routinely violated as thousands of people every day are denied entry into nations.

Thus, the right to freedom of movement is confined to that 'society' in which an individual can be a 'moral and legal unit'. As long as rights remain entrenched in geopolitical borders, the concepts of universalism and cosmopolitanism remain as abstract as were when they were first conceived of in the eighteenth century.

GEORGINA KRAUSE

ARTICLE 14
THE RIGHT TO ASYLUM: THE CASE OF JULIAN ASSANGE

"(1) Everyone has the right to seek and to enjoy in other countries asylum from persecution.
(2) This right may not be invoked in the case of prosecutions genuinely arising from non-political crimes or from acts contrary to the purposes and principles of the United Nations."

While the Universal Declaration of Human Rights (UDHR) does not constitute binding international law, in the area of refugee protection, Article 14 of the UDHR can be seen as a foundation stone of later binding treaties and provisions. [1] Article 14(1) provides the general right of asylum; Article 14(2) is an "*exclusion provision*" outlining circumstances where there is an exception to this rule.[2]

Considering this right and exclusion provision in the modern context brings up the contemporary question of the case of Julian Assange, the Australian national seeking asylum in the Ecuadorian embassy in London at the time of print. Assange, the founder of 'Wikileaks', fears persecution by the US government for related charges, a consequence of which he fears could be the death penalty. While likely charges in the US would thus be based upon what he considers a political crime (therefore not lying within the 14(2) exclusion), he could still be extradited to the US via Sweden in the following process. If arrested by UK officials, he would likely be extradited to Sweden where he faces charges of sexual assault, a serious *non-political* crime. Assange fears that the USA would exert enough political pressure to force Sweden into passing him over, resulting in him facing *political* persecution.

Ecuador granted Assange political asylum on the grounds that his fears of political persecution were reasonable. Thus, Ecuador is granting him asylum to protect him from potential extradition to the USA where he would likely face charges for political crimes, which lie outside the exclusion provision of Article 14(2) (and outside much of international law's other provisions on the matter). Ecuador's Ministry of Foreign Affairs, Trade And Integration statement consequent to this decision outlines their consideration of the potential for him to become: "a victim of political persecution, as a consequence of his determined defense to freedom of expression and freedom of press, as well as his position of condemn to the abuses that the power infers in different countries".[3]

However, while Ecuador has granted asylum, the UK has made it impossible for Assange to leave the Embassy. While the Embassy is technically Ecuadorian territory, and thus off limits for UK police, the second he leaves he is liable to be arrested for contravening his bail conditions. The UK would therefore be able to extradite him to Sweden. Ecuador is currently seeking a commitment from the UK government that it would refuse to support Sweden extraditing Assange onwards to the US, but there has been

---

[1] For example, the UN Refugee Convention (1951) and relevant human rights conventions such as the Covenant on Civil and Political Rights (1966).

[2] Kapferer, Sibylle. "Article 14(2) of the Universal Declaration of Human Rights and Exclusion from International Refugee Protection." *Refugee Survey Quarterly* 27.3 (2008): 53-75.

[3] "Ministry of Foreign Affairs, Trade and Integration of Ecuador." *Ministry of Foreign Affairs, Trade and Integration of Ecuador*. Web. 11 April 2013. <http://www.mmrree.gob.ec/eng/2012/com042.asp>.

no success in this area.[4] The situation almost seems to fall into one of legal stalemate. The question of what Assange's rights are is a complicated one. Even if, as he argues, the Swedish charges are politically motivated, whether he can avoid trial for a serious non-political crime certainly does not fall under basic 'human rights'. However, the problem remains that if he were to be given up for this, even if found innocent for these crimes, he could be prosecuted in America on political charges. Hence, Ecuador sees itself as protecting his human rights by preventing this from happening, while the UK would be fulfilling alternate legal obligations to extradite him to Sweden. This highlights the continuing problem of conflict at the overlap of the political, legal, and human rights spheres. This case, as many such cases, will likely be solved via political negotiations, as the uncertainty surrounding the legality of all sides makes a legal agreement unlikely. Assange's fate will most likely lie with the outcome of continued diplomatic negotiation.

---

[4] Quinn, Ben. "Ecuador Raises Julian Assange Case with Labour." *The Guardian*. Guardian News and Media, 29 March 2013. Web. 11 April 2013. <http://www.guardian.co.uk/media/2013/mar/30/ecuador-julian-assange-labour>.

ELIZABETH STOUT

ARTICLE 15
WHEN ARBITRARY BECOMES DANGEROUS

"(1) Everyone has the right to a nationality.
(2) No one shall be arbitrarily deprived of his nationality nor denied the right to change his nationality."

Article 15 remains crucial to the current state of international society, where peoples are physically divided by the state which they live in and the nationality that they possess. It is most relevant to current events, and will likely remain so for the considerable future. With an increasing flow of refugees as a result of conflicts in Syria, Libya and many vulnerable countries,[1] it would seem that the issue of changing nationality is one that is incredibly pressing, and must be dealt with so that people may be able to live in a way that best enables their rights to be fulfilled.

However, the present situation of the international community seems entirely inconsistent with a tightening of refugee laws in many countries.[2] It would seem that to allow that people be freely able to change their nationality, governments would be making a number of compromises they do not feel able to make. Article 15 does not place restrictions on which nationality a person may change to. It does not hold a requirement of certain skills in exchange for the right to change nationality. It does not suggest that such a change in nationality will be subject to a strict selection process.

But most importantly, what Article 15 does not do is define what it means by 'arbitrarily.' In failing to do this, it allows for all the above interpretations of the Article to be legislated for.

Granted, the Universal Declaration of Human Rights is not binding law. Governments would be entitled not to adhere to it even without the loophole that is the word 'arbitrary.' But this loophole allows that immigration laws are not seen to be in violation of human rights. It would appear then, that if a reason is given for the prevention of a particular person obtaining a particular nationality, this precludes the prevention from being arbitrary.

It is true that the drafters of the Universal Declaration may not have intended the free movement between borders that is now largely seen as both unattainable and undesirable. However, in asserting the Article to apply that '(e)veryone' have the right to a nationality, and 'no one' be arbitrarily denied the right to change theirs, Article 15 was certainly not intended to allow for a process of selection based perhaps on skill or on the level of trauma experienced in the evacuated country of the individual. It cannot be said to have been intended to allow the treatment that refugees so often experience in trying to change their nationality.

It is often said that a more developed and democratic state will be less prone to human rights violations. While this may hold truth with regard to some rights, concerning the right to change nationality developed countries may unfortunately be seen to violate Article 15 daily. In observing the situation in the UK, we see the example of Marjorie. Marjorie was a political activist in Uganda, teaching women about their rights, and to read

[1] "Number of Syrian Refugees Reaches 1 Million Mark." *United Nations High Commissioner for Refugees.* 6 March 2013. Web. 24 April 2013. <http://www.unhcr.org/513625ed6.html>.

[2] Syal, Rajeev. "Diane Abbott warns Labour on Immigration." *The Guardian.* 21 April 2013. Web. 25 April 2013. <http://www.guardian.co.uk/uk/2013/apr/21/diane-abbott-miliband-immigration>.

and write. Because of this, she was imprisoned twice. She says of her experience: "The horror that I experienced in there, you wouldn't wish that on anyone, not even your enemy. I was tortured, I was raped, I was burnt with cigarettes, I was cut with razors, electric shocks: all the horrible things you can think of to get information from someone."[3] She fled to the UK to escape her persecution, where she was greeted with a refusal of asylum. Eventually, after 6 years of fighting her case, she was given leave to remain.[4] To many people such a refusal would indeed appear arbitrary. Indeed, the very definition of arbitrary is that it is based on random choice or personal whim, rather than any reason or system. While these are undoubtedly systems, they would also appear to be based on such personal whim: on what abuse is deemed to be worst, by those assessing claims for asylum, and on which individuals are deemed to be telling the truth, based on the perceptions of those providing the inquisition. Debora Singer, Policy and Research Manager at Asylum Aid tells us that "(t)he Home Office seems to struggle with asylum claims that have any gender dimension. We know that woman (sic) are routinely, arbitrarily disbelieved by officials when they explain what has happened to them. We know that women are more likely than men to see asylum decisions overturned on appeal, so woeful is Home Office decision-making. And we know that the government hasn't honoured its promise to introduce meaningful gender-sensitive reforms."[5] Such treatment can clearly be regarded as arbitrary. But clearly also, in the eyes of the UK government, it is deemed necessary.

Thus we note a failing of the Universal Declaration of Human Rights. To be open to such extensive interpretation is to be open to a great departure from intent. It may be argued that the word 'arbitrary' was included in the Article in order that the courts of any particular time may use their own judgments regarding what is possible at that time. Thus international society, and individual governments within it, have created immigration laws in order to represent what they deem as practical at that time.

This seems to be what those formulating the policies assert. However, there is a marked inconsistency in this. Indeed, observing current necessity on immigration laws and what is currently deemed practical, one might as well be observing two completely separate issues. However, the two cannot be separated. Unfortunately, we live in an international community where allowances are not made for the political vulnerability of states outside our own. That Article 15 would apply to everyone equally becomes a fallacy in the face of government refusals to extend what is practical. It is a great failing of Article 15 that it does not possess the tools with which to change this. Herein lies a situation in which the arbitrary becomes dangerous.

---

[3] "Stories." *Women for Refugee Women.* Web. 24 April 2013. <http://www.refugeewomen.com/index.php/resources/stories>.

[4] Ibid.

[5] "Refused: The Experiences of Women Denied Asylum in the UK." *Women for Refugee Women.* Web. 25 April 2013. <http://www.refugeewomen.com/index.php/resources/publications>.

ANKITA SAXENA
AGED 17

ARTICLE 16
MARRIAGE AND THE FAMILY: FREE FROM THE PATRIARCHY?

"(1)Men and women of full age, without any limitation due to race, nationality or religion, have the right to marry and to found a family. They are entitled to equal rights as to marriage, during marriage and at its dissolution. (2) Marriage shall be entered into only with the free and full consent of the intending spouses. (3) The family is the natural and fundamental group unit of society and is entitled to protection by society and the State."

The brutal gang rape of Jyoti Singh Pandey on 16 December 2012 has stirred up the streets of Delhi into open rebellion, and the seats of the Parliament into open debate. In a country where sexism against females begins at birth, and a woman is raped every 21 minutes,[1] such action is crucial and highly called for. Whilst it will not take long to change the laws surrounding this, it will take many years to subdue the patriarchy and misogyny which is stifling the women of the world's tenth largest economy.[2] Jyoti may become symbolic of the vulnerability Indian women, and her death may be a trigger for increased awareness, but the traditional attitudes of much of the population cannot be changed as fast as the headlines. Indeed, with her rape leading to increased restrictions upon women, including recommendations for them to marry at an earlier age, are efforts to achieve Article 16 being stifled by a patriarchy?

In many respects Jyoti, a physiotherapy student and call centre worker, represented a new generation of Indian women. President Pranab Mukherjee described her as a 'symbol of all that new India strives to be',[3] and her father said: "(M)y daughter taught me...girls should be strong...should be independent...should have the strength to fight."[4] In life, Jyoti may have been a symbol for the freedom of Indian women but her death has inadvertently triggered increased restrictions and curfews for them. In the state Uttarkhand, the government has stopped women in public and private sector jobs working after 6 p.m,[5] and in another state there have been suggestions for girls to wear overcoats, or get married at an earlier age. The secretary of the All India Democratic Women's Association (AIDWA) Kavita Krishna said: "It's not just fear about

---

1 Chamberlain, Gethin. "'If Girls Look Sexy, Boys Will Rape.' Is This What Indian Men Really Believe?" *The Guardian.* 23 March 2013. Web. 17 April 2013. <http://www.guardian.co.uk/world/2013/mar/24/india-rape-disturbing-attitudes-men>.

2 "Brazilian Economy Overtakes UK's, Says CEBR." *BBC News.* 26 December 2011. Web. 17 April 2013. <http://www.bbc.co.uk/news/business-16332115>.

3 "Indian President Speaks out against Rape." *Al Jazeera.* 25 January 2013. Web. 17 April 2013. <http://www.aljazeera.com/news/asia/2013/01/201312519271678273 5.html>.

4 Schultz, Sandra and Wieland Wagner. "Rape Tragedy in India: Dreams of 'the Fearless One'." *Spiegal Online.* 25 January 2013. Web. 17 April 2013. <http://www.spiegel.de/international/world/exploring-the-lives-of-the-rape-victim-and-suspects-in-india-a-879187-2.html>.

5 "Uttarakhand Govt. Prohibits Women from Working beyond 6 P.m." *Yahoo! News India.* 12 January 2013. Web. 17 April 2013. <http://in.news.yahoo.com/uttarakhand-govt-prohibits-women-working-beyond-6-p-075323919.html>.

safety. It is an excuse to impose lots of patriarchal structures."[6] This so called 'patriarchal' culture condemns the women rather than the men, imposing restrictions on them rather then penalties on their attackers. Conservative politicians have ludicrously blamed girls' clothing,[7] such as Westerns skirts and high heels, for the rape incidents, whilst a Hindu guru, Ansarum Bapu, claimed that if Jyoti had called one her attackers, 'brother' she would have been safe - a statement so disillusioned it casts a negative light on the great influences of religion in the country.[8]

There is much social stigma surrounding rape, as many women do not report cases of sexual abuse for fear this will make them less marriageable - an attitude reminiscent of Victorian England. Such culture is so imprinted on the minds of Indians, that sexual abuse is not the only atrocity women face. In some states, there are only 830 women to every 1000 men,[9] owing to infanticide, childhood neglect, problems relating to dowry and domestic violence. Sagarika Ghose, a writer for the Hindustan Times, said: "A profound...almost pathological, hatred of women who aspires to be anything more than a mother and wife is justified on the grounds of tradition."[10]

However, unlike countries in the Middle- and Far-East, India is a democracy, and when masses of people crowd the streets of New Delhi demanding change, even the most corrupt politicians cannot turn a blind eye. Provoked by the state's reaction, the retired Justice Minister, JS Verma, ran a commission to review the laws in place regarding sexual abuse. Published on January 23, the commission recommended many changes, some of which India's government has approved.[11] Rampant sexual misconduct, such as 'eve-teasing', stalking and disrobing have been transformed from the pastimes of young men into actual crimes, and child trafficking has been officially banned. There are, however, some issues which have not been addressed. Currently, people in the military are tried in special courts so they are rarely prosecuted for sexual crimes;[12] whilst Verma suggested they be reverted to civilian courts, the government did not comply. Another great loophole

---

[6] Bhowmick, Nilanjana. "The Real Shame: India's Patriarchy Roars Back After Delhi Gang Rape." *Time World.* 18 January 2013. Web. 17 April 2013.<http://world.time.com/2013/01/18/the-real-shame-indias-patriarchy-roars-back-after-delhi-gang-rape/>.

[7] Chamberlain, Gethin. "'If Girls Look Sexy, Boys Will Rape.' Is This What Indian Men Really Believe?" *The Guardian.* 23 March 2013. Web. 17 April 2013. <http://www.guardian.co.uk/world/2013/mar/24/india-rape-disturbing-attitudes-men>.

[8] Adams Otis, Ginger. "Swami claims Indian rape victim was 'as guilty' as her attackers." *NYDailyNews.* 7 January 2013. Web. 17 April 2013. <http://www.nydailynews.com/news/world/swami-blames-rape-victim-article-1.1234924>.

[9] "India's Unwanted Girls." *BBC News.* 23 May 2011. Web. 27 April 2013. <http://www.bbc.co.uk/news/world-south-asia-13331808>.

[10] Ghose, Sagarika. "Time to Make a Choice." *Hindustan Times.*8 January 2013. Web. 17 April 2013. <http://www.hindustantimes.com/editorial-views-on/SagarikaGhose/Time-to-make-a-choice/Article1-986871.aspx> .

[11] "Verma Panel Submits Report on Rape Laws." *Hindustan Times.* 23 January 2013. Web. 17 April 2013. <http://www.hindustantimes.com/India-news/NewDelhi/Justice-Verma-submits-report-on-reforming-rape-laws-suggests-time-bound-trial/Article1-998567.aspx>.

[12] Ibid

in the law is the issue of marital rape. There is currently no legislation against this[13] - perhaps not surprising in a country where divorce is still not commonly accepted, and where the victim knows the offender in 93% of rape cases.[14] However, feminist groups such as AIDWA have been exerting great pressure on to the government to change this, and this issue is due to be discussed in the first half of India's Budget later this year. More promising than the alterations to the law is the 'the peaceful manner in which the protests were carried out,'[15] according to Justice Verma. He said: 'Youth has taught us what we, the older generation, were not aware of', and that he was 'struck by how the youth rose to the occasion.'[16]

Youth may be the solution to the problem, but may also be at the root of it. The underlying issue is not simply gender inequality but social inequality. Many of the men who commit these crimes are often from poor backgrounds,[17] and in a city like Delhi, the contrast between the gated mansions and the doorless slums are particularly stark. One of the main issues here is that most of the residents are migrants from neighbouring North-Indian states, such as Haryana, where the attitudes towards women are especially regressive. Social circumstances cannot make these crimes in any way excusable, but merely illustrate that in order for there to be real progress in this country, the deep cracks beneath the gaze of the wealthy politicians must be mended.

The slogan of Jyoti's old school is: "Education opens the door, but you must enter yourself."[18] There have been great changes in India following 16 December, which have certainly 'opened the doors' to a fresh outlook on the serious problems Indian women still have to face every day. However, it is too early to judge if the general public is prepared to confront issues like the lack of wealth and aspiration of the youth in Delhi, or if people still only see the smaller picture, from the keyhole in the door. It is too early to judge if Jyoti Singh will become symbolic of Indian reform, or if she will simply remain a sad reminder of the vulnerability and oppression of women in this rapidly modernising but innately sexist country.

---

[13] Nelson, Dean. "Men Can Still Rape Their Wives in India After New Government Bill." *The Telegraph.* 14 March 2013. Web. 17 April 2013. <http://www.telegraph.co.uk/news/worldnews/asia/india/9930838/Men-can-still-rape-their-wives-in-India-after-new-Government-bill.html>.

[14] "Danger is near: 99% victims in Tamil Nadu knew their rapists." *The Times of India.* 7 January 2013. Web. 17 April 2013. <http://articles.timesofindia.indiatimes.com/2013-01-07/chennai/36191609_1_sexual-abuse-victims-sexual-assault>.

[15] "Verma Panel Submits Report on Rape Laws." *Hindustan Times.* 23 January 2013. Web. 17 April 2013. <http://www.hindustantimes.com/India-news/NewDelhi/Justice-Verma-submits-report-on-reforming-rape-laws-suggests-time-bound-trial/Article1-998567.aspx>.

[16] "Justice JS Verma submits report on rape laws, 'shocked' by system's apathy" *Times of India.* 23 January 2013. Web. 17 April 2013 <http://articles.timesofindia.indiatimes.com/2013-01-23/india/36504469_1_sexual-offences-home-secretary-justice-js-verma>.

[17] Mahr, Krista. "Another High Profile Rape in India Highlights Ongoing Problem." *World Time.* 18 March 2013. Web. 17 April 2013. <http://world.time.com/2013/03/18/another-high-profile-rape-in-india-highlights-ongoing-problem/>.

[18] Schultz, Sandra and Wieland Wagner. "Rape Tragedy in India: Dreams of 'the Fearless One'." *Spiegal Online.* 25 January 2013. Web. 17 April 2013. <http://www.spiegel.de/international/world/exploring-the-lives-of-the-rape-victim-and-suspects-in-india-a-879187-2.html>.

Nick Roberts

Article 17
A Worthy Addition?

"(1) Everyone has the right to own property alone as well as in association with others. (2) No one shall be arbitrarily deprived of his property."

Property, and the right to it, has been used as a justification for many of the worst excesses of human society. Inequality, war, and the hideous mark on Western civilisation that was slavery have all been defended on the grounds that an individual has the right to own and defend their property. It would seem incredible then that this tool of oppression has been codified in Article 17 of the Universal Declaration of Human Rights. While Article 4 inhibits the return of slavery and various other United Nations regulations strictly govern the case for war,[1] inequality is imperfectly addressed by any of the other 30 Articles. All humans are born equal but only on vary rare occasions do they die that way. Indeed, thanks to the right of everyone to own property and not be arbitrarily deprived of it, humans remain equal for such a small fragment of time after birth that it may be questioned whether or not Article 17 directly contradicts the inspirational figurehead of the Declaration that is Article 1.

Article 17 must be viewed, perhaps more than any other, within the context of its inception. 1948 saw the very inception of a Cold War not yet begun and critics of the UDHR have cited this as evidence that the Declaration was little more than American propaganda.[2] Its critics claim that it attempted to highlight the difference in civil liberty between the 'land of the free', which, let us not forget, was still facing severe problems of racial inequality and segregation at home, and the oppressive Stalinist regime of the USSR. Many of the provisions were destined to highlight differences between the two blocs, although this was not quite so evident at its inception. Alexandre Bogomolov represented the Soviet Union on the Commission on Human Rights though apparently was unable to direct the draft in order to suitably impress senior figures in Moscow; the USSR, Belarus, Czechoslovakia, Yugoslavia, Poland, and Ukraine all abstained from signing the UDHR.

Another key facet in the admission of Article 17 must be the influence of the Constitution of the United States of America. Chaired by an American, Eleanor Roosevelt, and Vice-Chaired by a member of the Chinese Guomidang, whose political ideology was heavily influenced by American constitutionalism, the Commission on Human Rights was undoubtedly ready to accommodate some lessons learned from its 1787 predecessor, though Dr Peng Chun Chang did urge the removal of all references to God and nature in order to encourage universalism. Importantly, one value which is enshrined in the US Constitution above all others is that of the right to private property. The political system, with its acclaimed checks and balances, was designed to stop a wave of public support bringing a radical government to power in America which, in the nightmare scenario envisaged by the Founding Fathers, would then proceed to arbitrarily deprive the members of this landed aristocracy of their property. The indirect election of the President and the

---

1 "Charter, United Nations, Chapter I, Purposes and Principles." *UN News Center*. UN. Web. 25 April 2013. <http://www.un.org/en/documents/charter/chapter1.shtml>.

2 Hussein Shaban, Abdul. "Human Rights: An American Weapon." *Middle East Monitor.* Web. 25 April 2013. <http://www.middleeastmonitor.com/articles/middle-east/5725-human-rights-an-american-weapon>.

Senate, the lack of nominating conventions, and the separation of powers were intended to keep this élite in control of American politics and maintain the staunch defence of private property. Inequality has followed. Private property inhibits equality, just as it often inhibits true progress. Arbitrary removal of private property fuelled the French Revolution, yet, despite its chaotic violence, the proceedings of 1789 eventually gave way to a proposed Jacobin constitution which guaranteed universal suffrage, regardless of gender, wealth, or political preference, a proposal which would have been impossible in the feudal, monarchical France of the ancien régime. This constitution was eventually delayed by the pressures of war. Across Europe, as well as in East Asia, the arbitrary removal of property, or land reform to give it its socially acceptable name, helped to break down centuries-old feudal ties and establish a new, increasingly democratic trend. America, lacking a feudal past, never had to overcome these obstacles and, perhaps, does not appreciate the oppressive side of the right to property. Either way, it would be wrong to say that the right to private property has been a cornerstone of Western democracy and its protection does not deserve a place alongside the more prescient and necessary provisions of the UDHR.

The example of Article 17 serves to illustrate the dynamic nature of Human Rights. In the context of the beginnings of the Cold War, faced with a conflict with revolutionary, revisionist, communist powers, the maintenance of private property appeared to be an essential road block to this totalitarian system. However, in the post-Cold War era, this must be re-evaluated. Private property is no longer a road block to a dead ideology, it is instead a road block to equality of person and many of the other rights enshrined in the UDHR. As the world develops and changes, so must the UDHR progress, otherwise it will be left behind, a fate that would represent great tragedy for human society.

C.M.K. DJORDJEVIC

ARTICLE 18
THE IMPORTANCE OF CHOICE

"Everyone has the right to freedom of thought, conscience and religion; this right includes freedom to change his religion or belief, and freedom, either alone or in community with others and in public or private, to manifest his religion or belief in teaching, practice, worship and observance."

This is one of the most essential statements within the Universal Declaration of Human Rights because it enables an individual qua herself to choose her own conception of the good and her own relationship to the Sublime (even if that is no relationship). It holds out the firm belief that, beneath the cultural contexts and embedded practices of our community, we are persons with the right (and ability) to choose for ourselves. This has been deeply misunderstood in recent years, I would argue.

To illustrate how this is meant to work, the story of a book and a translator will be very useful. The book is Hume's *Dialog Concerning Natural Religions* and the translator is radical German thinker Johann Hamann.

Hume's book, still controversial today, is an attack on religion as the expression of a divine order. For Hume- and Dawkins takes much from Hume - a god of reason may well be a giant spider (in the parlance of our times, a flying spaghetti monster). The book shows the absurdity of trying to argue for a 'clockmaker' god.

Now, lest the reader misunderstand why this example, let us talk about the first German translation. In the heady days of Germany's enlightenment, as Kant and Mendelssohn debated - in a deeply respectful way - Jewish theology, as young Hegel prepared for his schooling, and as the light of reason positioned itself firmly against anything contingent and cultural, an odd thing happened. A brilliant literary critic named Hamann went to England for some business. During his trip, he had a felt vision of G-d. And he came to realize - much as Pascal before and Kierkegaard and Wittgenstein after - that the true meaning of religion was not in the logical puttering of arguments or with the hair-splitting legalism of canonical law. It was meant as a condition for relating directly to G-d as an individual person.

To reaffirm, before I press on, imagine if Martin Luther had translated Sam Harris's *End of Faith* or if St. Thomas Aquinas had quoted at length from *Breaking the Spell.* "Odd thought!" the reader may scoff. But, sadly, up until our century, such things were not unthinkable departures from dogmatic understandings but necessary conditions for thought itself (Aquinas is a good example. You would be hard pressed to find a more rational, charitable and honest reconstruction of paganism).

Hamann translated Hume's book precisely because belief without question is not belief at all. The UN declaration affirms two facts that, I think, our above historical sketch shows quite well. (1) One must be as free and unencumbered to choose one's own conception of the good, interdependently (or as much so as possible) from coercive elements of one's community. (2) Any position that precludes this possibility of choice is not respectful of the full dignity of a human being as a being capable of choice.

Hamann's insight, more true today than ever, is that to be fully human and capable of a relationship with the Sublime, one must be a being capable of choice in the richest sense of the term. The Universal Declaration affirms this.

RAPHAELLA PITT

ARTICLE 18
THE CENTREPIECE OF THE UNIVERSAL DECLARATION OF HUMAN RIGHTS

A lot of importance and focus, similarly media attention, is placed on the articles of the Universal Declaration of Human Rights (UDHR) which have a legalistic nature, such as Article 11 on the right to a fair trial, or Article 6 on the right for every person to be treated equally under the law. However, it is Article 18 that is the foundation of these rights and arguably without it, no other rights would be possible.

Article 18 can essentially be split into two distinct parts, the right to freedom of thought and conscience and the right to freedom of religion. The Declaration states those rights that all states should uphold in order not to fall foul of humanity. Without the fundamental right to freedom of thought and conscience, we have nothing else; not a free trial, not punishment, nor in fact laws. All these legalistic elements of society come from a thought process by an individual at a particular time. It is this conscience which marks us out as homo sapiens and separates us from other mammals. Thus violations of this right must seen as the most serious of all and should receive the most attention and uproar since this is an infringement of a right that makes us man.

Without this right the horrors accounted in modern classical novels would be realized. Society that men like Orwell feared so greatly would materialize in a heartbeat. The epitome of such novels and almost Armageddon predictions is that of 1984 by George Orwell which illustrates, with chilling accuracy, what a futuristic, totalitarian state without thought and conscience would be like. As he states in his book, the right to freedom of conscience is such a part of humanity that the state's position is that "until they [the people] became conscious they will never rebel, and until after they have rebelled they cannot become conscious"[1]. This chilling quotation describes how necessary this right is to humanity, not only in terms of the ability it gives us to express ourselves and 'rebel' as he puts it, but also what marks us out as autonomous individuals.

The tragedy is that in 2013, 29 years after Orwell's predicted society, grave violations of this intrinsic right can be seen across the globe in the form of dictatorships. Though history has ended some of these, it still exists in the Democratic People's Republic of Korea. This totalitarian regime controls all mediums by which one could be influenced to cultivate a thought against the state such as a restricted Google and state-controlled television. Additionally for the vast majority of the population access to the internet is but a dream and for those who can use it, access is extremely limited. By limiting these modes of communication and discovery, one's thoughts and conscience are profoundly limited. This is the most grave of breaches since citizens of that nation are living not as autonomous agents but as mere shells of man filled with the ideology of the state.

Therefore without this freedom, humanity would be without democracy and human rights. This is why it should be staunchly and severely protected for as Benjamin Franklin states "without freedom of thought there can be no such thing as wisdom"[2], wisdom being an undoubted necessity of human development.

The second strand of the Article is the right to freedom of religion, including the right to change it or to manifest it as one sees fit. Religion forms an integral part of the

---

[1] Orwell, George. *1984: A Novel*. New York: Signet Classic, 1977.

[2] Franklin, Benjamin. "Letter from Silence Dogood." The New-England Courant, Boston, Massachusetts, 1722.

identity of many and so one has arguably an intrinsic right to it. Religion is intertwined with most elements of modern civic society and so to limit it in any shape or form is highly contentious. This influence is made clear from law to which social norms are accepted, such as couples being unable to touch before marriage in certain sects of Judaism. As warped as the following statement by Weinberg is, it demonstrates how religion has become part of all that we do, even the morality of our actions or the actions themselves, for "good people do good things and bad people do bad things. But for good people to do bad things, that takes religion"[3].

The UDHR seeks to enshrine in a document the rights that every man on earth should enjoy. Religion is undoubtedly one of those rights. However it is also one that is violated time after time. One of the ultimate violations being in Sharia Law countries such as Iran, where the right to change one's belief, dictated in the UDHR, amounts to apostasy which in turn amounts to death. This limitation upon man's rights, to the extent of criminalizing it, is a severe and shocking infringement not only upon freedom of religion, but also upon freedom of thought, which governed that departure from the religious norm. Though it is easy to talk of violations in distant countries, infringements upon this central right can be seen far closer to home.

Manifesting one's religion is routinely called into question in Europe as a whole. Recent case law merely illustrates this fact. From the BA flight attendant in 2010 being prevented from visibly wearing a cross (which the European Court of Human Rights recently found to be a violation of this right) to across the channel, the ban in France of the full-faced veil, worn by many Islamic women. This is prejudice. Removing religion and having a face of being more sectarian in the public sphere is a clear and unequivocal violation of Article 18. In response to said violations, the UN has created the office of the Special Rapporteur on the freedom of religion or belief. This independent expert appointed by the UN Human Rights Council demonstrates how important upholding and preserving this intrinsic right to religious freedom is. Therefore abuses of this, however small, cannot be ignored for if allowed, they could lead to a fast and slippery slope of complete secularization, or even as history has shown us, genocide.

Article 18 is necessary. The UDHR is necessary, as it has become essential in the modern world for such fundamental human rights to be enshrined in a document so they can be ratified and adhered to. Nothing should be imposed on man against their will. As Mandela, a champion of human rights, once stated, "for to be free is not merely to cast off one's chains but to live in a way that respects and enhances the freedom of others"[4]. In order to maintain a humanity we are proud of, the world must strive to preserve the rights declared by the UDHR especially article 18.

---

[3] In discussion with Richard Dawkins in 2009. Steven Weinberg is a Professor of Physics and Astronomy at University of Texas.

[4] Mandela, Nelson. *Long Walk to Freedom: The Autobiography of Nelson Mandela.* Boston: Little, Brown, 1994.

C.M.K. DJORDJEVIC

ARTICLE 19
THE ROLE OF DIGNITY

"Everyone has the right to freedom of opinion and expression; this right includes freedom to hold opinions without interference and to seek, receive and impart information and ideas through any media and regardless of frontiers."

The key to all human rights is the vague and seemingly empty idea of "human dignity." It is vague because any definition of it quickly falls in a circle. People are worthy of respect because they have dignity and people have dignity insofar as we treat them with respect. And it seems empty because it is not an empirical thing - dignity is not inherited in the same way genes are and is not in the world in the same way that protons are. And yet it is an essential concept for the idea project of human rights - indeed without it, saying things like "he acted inhumanely" would be senseless.

Part of the dignity of people is my respect for them as agents, as equals, as beings capable of thought. Without this, human beings are, at best, children to be taken care of by those of us with sufficient intelligence (prestige, money, etc.) to know what is best.

The most essential idea of equality has two distinct requirements. It requires that people, in the conditions of their lives, have enough to be able to think and enjoy their world. Further, though, it requires that people be allowed to say what they believe - even if it is in deep conflict with their fellows.

To restrict this ability is to dismiss someone's reasons for holding different beliefs than one's own. It immediately disregards their ability and, worse, their agency. It is to treat them as creatures that are less than human.

No one believes anything without some reason for it. And to simply not take this reason seriously is to not take someone's humanity seriously. It is a dangerous road to walk down.

Yan-Ho Lai [1]

Article 20
Systematic Violations of Right to Freedom of Assembly: A Case Study of Hong Kong

"(1)Everyone has the right to freedom of peaceful assembly and association. (2) No one may be compelled to belong to an association."

Introduction

The right to freedom of assembly is a fundamental right of every human being and is recognized in the Universal Declaration of Human Rights (UDHR). It is associated closely with freedom of expression and of thought. This fundamental right should be regarded as the prime value of a civilized modern society. However, even metropolitan cities often violate this right by their government system. This article aims at reviewing the implementation of right of freedom of assembly in Hong Kong, for the sake of displaying how legal and police systems violate the fundamental rights of expression over local citizens.

Conditioning right to freedom of assembly under Public Order Ordinance

Hong Kong is a Special Administrative Region (HKSAR) of People's Republic of China, which means its political, legal, economic and social systems are distinctive from China, according to the principle of 'One Country, Two Systems'. Indeed, the distinctiveness of its systems is a legacy of the British colonial system before the transfer of sovereignty to China in 1997. Its legal system is compatible with International Human Rights law to a limited extent, since the Basic Law (BL) and Bill of Rights Ordinance (BORO) in Hong Kong incorporate the International Covenant on Civil and Political Rights (ICCPR). However, revisions of Public Order Ordinance in 1997 were a step backward on the protection of right to freedom of assembly. I will first discuss the development of the Ordinance and its restrictions on public assembly, and then argue why conditioning right to freedom of assembly is a violation of human rights.

The Public Order Ordinance is the result of 1967 Riots, which was initiated by communist-affiliated labour unions in Hong Kong against Colonial Government, and it caused massive causalities. It was passed for the sake of suppression of the protestors in the Riots, and hence the stability of British rule. In 1980, the Government revised the ordinance that any public assembly carrying over 30 people or public demonstration with over 20 participants are compelled to notify the Police and to apply for a license, otherwise it would be a criminal offense. In 1995, before the transfer of sovereignty, the Colonial Government replaced the license system of the Public Order Ordinance with notification in

[1] Yan Ho LAI is the Convener of Civil Human Rights Front, Hong Kong in 2011/2012. The Front was established in 2002 for promoting civil and political rights and legislation against different forms of discriminations in the city. It also organizes the 1 July Rally, which is the annual demonstration with the largest number of participants in Hong Kong. He is now a Master Candidate in Political Sociology in London School of Economics and Political Science.

which no license of permission from Commissioner of Police is needed for public assembly. Yet, after 1997, the Provisional Legislative Council, which was set up without suffrage but by the Chinese Government, reverted to the abolished regulations in the Ordinance that any public assembly and demonstration without notice of no objection and its conditions by Commissioner of Police will be regarded as unlawful and/or unauthorized, and will be regarded as criminal offense on the part of participants and organizers.[2]

The system of notice of no objection (NNO) should be addressed as a violation of right to freedom of assembly. Section 7(1) of the Public Order Ordinance states that, a public meeting may take place only if the Commissioner of Police is notified and the holding of the meeting is not prohibited by the Commissioner.[3] Also, according to Section 8(5) the Commissioner of Police shall issue written acknowledgment of receipt of notice for the person giving or delivering the notice of public meeting.[4] The Commissioner of Police has power to prohibit public meeting if he/she thinks such prohibition is necessary in the interests of national security, public safety, public order or the protection of the rights and freedoms of others, in accordance to Section 9(1).[5] Moreover, Section 17(A) states that any public meeting or public procession which takes place in contravention of Section 7, which is aforementioned, shall be an unauthorized assembly.[6] In short, any person who would like to organize a legal public assembly must gain notice of no objection from Commissioner of Police. Otherwise, he/she is committing a criminal offense.

What implications we can find from the above restrictions of the Public Order Ordinance? The implications are twofold. Firstly, it conditions the right to freedom of assembly as a top-down entitlement, not basic equal rights. Second, it favors the state apparatus to prohibit the exercise of right to freedom of assembly.

The notice of no objection alienates the concept of right to freedom of assembly. According to a judgment of Final Court of Appeal in Hong Kong, the freedom of peaceful assembly is a fundamental right. It is closely associated with the fundamental right of the freedom of speech.[7] However, now police often use a "balance" approach to interpret public assembly and procession and as a consideration of issuing the NNO. They emphasize interests of non-demonstrators and users of public transport and highways rather than the rights of protestors, hence the levelling down of the right to freedom of assembly, which alienates its "fundamental" nature. Furthermore, under the procedure of NNO the exercise of right to freedom of assembly is determined by Police Commissioner

---

[2] Police Power Concern Group of Civil Human Rights Front, *Decoding Public Order Ordinance: From 97 to Wolf and Eagel* (* Wolf and Eagel represent the current Chief Executive and Commissioner of Police of Hong Kong respectivly), Hong Kong, Nov 2012, p.2.

[3] S.7 (1), Public Order Ordinance (Cap.245)

[4] S.8 (5), ibid.

[5] S.9 (1), ibid.

[6] S.17A, ibid.

[7] *Leung Kwok Hung & Others v HKSAR* [2005] 3 HKLRD 164

rather than individual citizens. The entitlement of the right is shifted from human dignity to decision of authority. This is certainly a violation of the right since the state manipulates the nature of basic, fundamental right of expression of free and equal human beings.

The second implication is linked with the language of the Public Order Ordinance. Any senior Police Officers have the rights to deem a public assembly or public procession unauthorized or unlawful, and to stop it. They can even prosecute participants when they consider the assembly generate public disorder, violations of freedom and interest of others, and national security. However, the regulation of the Public Order Ordinance on public assemblies and its offences of "unauthorized assembly", "unlawful assembly" and "disorder in public places" are too vaguely, broadly and subjectively defined, which could lead to arbitrary and selective prosecution of protestors.[8] For instance, according to a statistic conducted by a local group, at least 416 citizens were prosecuted in public procession and assembly in 2011, which broke the record since the 1967 Riots,[9] and is about 8 times more than in 2010 because of the large scale anti-budget protests of March 6th, the vigil protest of June 4th and the July 1st demonstration.[10] Furthermore, police laid charges under the ordinance against 45 protesters of "unauthorized assembly", "unlawful assembly" and "disorder in public places", compared with a total of 39 between 1997 and 2010.[11] The offenses above are criminal and can result in sentence. Such political prosecution is certainly a violation of right to freedom of assembly, and the ambiguous definitions of principles in the Ordinance indirectly allow the police force possible to exercise "discretion" to suppress public assembly.

Political Oppression by Police

The police force is regarded as part of the state apparatus in the oppression of civil rights. Hence, the right to freedom of assembly is suffering under state systematic violations.

First of all, the Hong Kong police frequently used pepper spray against demonstrators during petitions, public processions and meetings in recent years, sometimes without proper warnings and/or at short range. Sometimes peaceful protestors and even journalists nearby were sprayed and hurt by such sprays, used obviously for no good justifications. Such improper uses of force were at least reckless if not intentional, and in any case

---

[8] *Joint Submission by NGOs coordinated by the Hong Kong Human Rights Monitor to the UN Human Rights Committee on the implementation of the ICCPR in the Hong Kong Special Administration Region , China* (JSUNHRC) , Oct 2012, para.30.

[9] Civil Human Rights Front, *A Report on the Police Abuse of Power 2011*, January 2012.

[10] Human Rights Monitor, *ANNI Report 2012 on the performance of National Human Rights Institutions in Asia* (for Asian NGOs Network on National Human Rights Institution, ANNI), Nov 2012.

[11] "Record number prosecuted under tough protest law", *South China Morning Post*, 10 Nov 2012.

unlawful.[12] In a protest against the government budget of 2011, police used pepper spray against the protestors including a 9-year-old child.[13] Such usage was condemned as political threat against peaceful protestors.

Secondly, police used substantial barriers against demonstrators' rights to expression. In a recent instance, NGOs and some of the political parties held a demonstration on 30 June 2012 urging the Chinese President to investigate the suspicious death of Li Wangyang, a Chinese labour activist who participated in supporting June 4th in 1989 and was kept in jail for approximately 22 years. Despite the Appeal Board on Public Meetings and Processions of Hong Kong Police ruling that protesters could take up 40 meters of the path opposite to the hotel where President Hu stayed for demonstration, the police subsequently claimed that the ruling would seriously affect their security plan and they would therefore take corresponding action. They placed 2-metre tall water barriers weighing 2 tons at the perimeter to engulf and sealed off the protest area so that protestors, their placards and banners inside, were basically invisible to President Hu or anyone outside. Protesters could only look outside through the narrow gaps of the water barrier with a view of small angle. This measure defeats the intention by the Appeal Board to allow the demonstration to take place nearer to the Convention Centre and the hotel. When the protestors attempted to climb and confront the heavy barriers, the police fired powerful pepper spray, from bottles of the size of fire extinguishers. The police explained they had so acted to protect public safety. Yet civil society criticized the police for hiding their protests by use of water barriers and disproportionate force.[14]

Last but not least, the approaches against public assembly taken by the police are seemingly contrary to one of the judgments of Final Court of Appeal on the role of government in public assembly in Hong Kong. This judgment was published in 2005 in the *LEUNG Kwok-Hung* case, which refers to appeal on the constitutionality of regulations in public procession under the Public Order Ordinance.[15] According to the judgment, the court emphasized that the government has a positive duty in peaceful public assembly, with reference to a case at the European Court of Human Rights:

"Genuine, effective freedom of peaceful assembly cannot, therefore, be reduced to a mere duty on the part of the State not to interfere: a purely negative conception would not be compatible with the object and purpose of Article 11. Like Article 8 [right to respect for private and family life], Article 11 sometimes requires positive measures to be taken, even in the sphere of relations between individuals, if need be."[16]

---

[12] JSUNHRC, para. 29.

[13] Civil Human Rights Front, January 2012.

[14] Human Rights Monitor, Nov 2012.

[15] 3 HKLRD 164

[16] European Court of Human Rights, *Plattform 'Ärzte für das Leben' v. Austria* (1991) 13 EHRR 204, para. 32.

The government recognized their positive duty in public assembly and procession in the court,[17] yet the police often initiate obstacles against public assembly and procession. Apart from the use of pepper spray and huge barriers, police always blamed the protestors as disrupting public traffic and infringing the rights and interests of others. However, police are criticized for failing to order proper traffic arrangements during public procession, since they are the most resourceful authority to do so. Positive duty usually refers to facilitation and assistance of a party to another as obligation. However, the passivity of police in facilitating public assembly and public traffic creates conflicts between citizens and demonstrators, and it is a negative approach for public assembly.

In sum, the passive facilitation and progressive blockades of police in public procession and meetings hinder the right to freedom of assembly and legitimize the use of offensive measures against protestors.

Prospect: Protecting right to freedom of assembly by establishment or individuals?

It is obvious that establishment in Hong Kong cannot guarantee the right to freedom of assembly of citizens. On the contrary, the legal system and executive bodies infringe upon it. In addition, the lack of independent monitoring body against the Police Force worsens the situation. The Independent Police Complaint Council (IPCC) in Hong Kong cannot fulfill its monitoring role because of its limited mandate to observe, monitor and review the complaints handled by the Complaints Against Police Office (CAPO), which is an internal unit of the police forces. The IPCC's limited access to the information of police forces further undermines its effectiveness.[18] For example, the IPCC once requested that police provide documents on security order during the visit of Vice-Premier Li Keqiang in Aug 2011 to investigate whether police action and its arrangement were proportionate. However, the police refused to offer the relevant paper in the name of sensitive information. This response is suspected as an intention against the investigation.[19]

The civil society and citizens in Hong Kong should protect and promote the right to freedom of assembly themselves, when the establishment acts against their responsibility. In fact, many NGOs in Hong Kong keep organizing public assembly and processions as a way to exercise the right of assembly and expression continuously. They also publish pamphlets critically reviewing the current legal system, particularly the Public Order Ordinance, and the right to freedom of assembly in the city.[20] These show not only resistance and challenge to the existing hindrance and violations of the right to freedom of assembly, but also a civic education for citizens in order to encourage them to join the force for human rights.

Actions are protections. Only by exercising our right to freedom of assembly can we resist the violations of the system and promote the expansion of this basic right of

---

[17] Ibid, para. 23.

[18] JSUNHRC, para. 31.

[19] Police Power Concern Group of Civil Human Rights Front, p. 8.

[20] Please refer to the images attached in the article.

expression. The road to full utilization of Universal Declaration of Human Rights is far from reached, but is our responsibility to achieve.

Demonstration Against the Abuse of Police Power in Preventing the Freedom of Public Assembly

Joseph Brown

Article 21
The Will of the People? Forcible Disappearances in Syria

"(1) Everyone has the right to take part in the government of his country, directly or through freely chosen representatives. (2) Everyone has the right of equal access to public service in his country.
(3) The will of the people shall be the basis of the authority of government; this will shall be expressed in periodic and genuine elections which shall be by universal and equal suffrage and shall be held by secret vote or by equivalent free voting procedures."

As of October 2012, up to 28,000 Syrians had disappeared, having been taken from the streets, often forcibly abducted at the hands of government troops or security forces.[1] This number is rising. It is a bleak story being told by human rights groups on the ground in Syria. Relatives are unable to discover the fate of their loved ones. Many of those abducted are undoubtedly dead. Others are being held in prisons or secret detention centres.[2] Human rights groups have suggested torture to be rife during interrogations here.[3] The global campaign network Avaaz has released what has been described as 'a harrowing film'[4], illustrating the realities of the conflict through footage of the forced disappearances. We see three soldiers grab two women who are walking down a street. They are beaten, then dragged out of view.

The Campaign Director for Avaaz, Alice Jay, tells us that: "Syrians are being plucked off the street by Syrian security forces and paramilitaries and being 'disappeared' into torture cells. Whether it is women buying groceries or farmers going for fuel, nobody is safe."[5] Such is the case of Abd al-Akram al-Sakka, a 67-year-old imam who is believed to have been missing for over a year. Despite the desperate pleas of his family, no information as to his location nor his condition have been disclosed.[6]

And Wissam Araji, who, at the time of print, has been missing for over two years.

---

[1] Harding, Luke. "Up to 28,000 Syrians Have 'disappeared' since Uprising Began." *The Guardian.* 18 October 2012. Web. 25 April 2013. <http://www.guardian.co.uk/world/2012/oct/18/28000-syrians-disappeared-uprising>.

[2] Ibid

[3] "Kept in the Dark - The Murky World if Enforced Disappearances." *Amnesty International.* 29 August 2012. Web. 25 April 2013. <http://www.amnesty.org/en/news/kept-dark-murky-world-enforced-disappearances-2012-08-28>.

[4] Ibid

[5] Harding, Luke. "Up to 28,000 Syrians Have 'disappeared' since Uprising Began." *The Guardian.* 18 October 2012. Web. 25 April 2013. <http://www.guardian.co.uk/world/2012/oct/18/28000-syrians-disappeared-uprising>.

[6] "Syria Urged to End Forced Disappearances." *Amnesty International USA.* 29 August 2012. Web. 25 April 2013. <http://www.amnestyusa.org/news/press-releases/syria-urged-to-end-enforced-disappearances-1>.

His family now fear for their own safety, as well as for his.[7]

These disappearances are the result of a people protesting for the right to participate in their own government. It is a right guaranteed to them in Article 21 of the Universal Declaration of Human Rights. Article 21 states that 'the will of the people shall be the basis of the authority of government' and it is on this basis that David Cameron called on the National Security Council to discuss the conflict in Syria.[8] Senior UK ministers considered the military, humanitarian and diplomatic options for dealing with the violence and the growing refugee crisis. This Council resulted in the recognition of Syria's opposition coalition as the sole legitimate representative of the Syrian people. Western powers have been reluctant to intervene in this politically charged uprising, but this recognition has signalled a change in policy; a recognition of the violation of Article 21 that has set the tone for more serious UN discussion of the conflict.

Opposition and human rights activists estimate that, as of November 2012, more than 36,000 people have been killed since the uprising against President Assad's rule began in March 2011,[9] which asks, with increasing urgency, should the West intervene in Syria? If its commitment to Article 21 and the UDHR in general is as bulletproof as the West would profess, then action is obligatory in order to defend this pillar of the democratic world.

---

[7] Macleod, Hugh and Annasofie Flamand. "Wave of Enforced Disappearances in Syria." *Al-Jazeera.* 24 April 2011. Web. 25 April 2013. <http://www.aljazeera.com/news/middleeast/2011/04/2011424201513361740.html>.

[8] "Syria Conflict: William Hague to Meet Opposition Leaders." *BBC News: Politics.* 15 November 2012. Web. 25 April 2013. <http://www.bbc.co.uk/news/uk-politics-20335346> .

[9] "Syria Civil War 'Kills 36,000'." *The Telegraph.* 31 October 2012. Web. 25 April 2013. <http://www.telegraph.co.uk/news/worldnews/middleeast/syria/9645076/Syria-civil-war-kills-36000.html>.

MICHAEL PEARSON

ARTICLE 22
A HUE OF CONFORMITY

"Everyone, as a member of society, has the right to social security and is entitled to realization, through national effort and international co-operation and in accordance with the organization and resources of each State, of the economic, social and cultural rights indispensable for his dignity and the free development of his personality."

The free development of personality is a right that individuals should be free to pursue in whichever way they see fit. Throughout life, the development of our personality is influenced by many factors; parents, friends, social groups, society. However, for an external body to force constraints upon individuals, which leave members of society no choice as to conform to a particular way of living, is an affront to the rights of individuals. Clearly, there are certain constraints upon individuals that are imposed by external bodies that are necessary to maximise the liberty of all members of society. It should be a criminal offence to murder. It should be a criminal offence to rape. These are instances to constrain individuals from committing direct harm to others in society. However, in the spirit of John Stuart Mill, past this, the state has no business from forcing individuals to conform to an ideology or a way of life as this significantly impacts on the cognitive ability of members of society to explore their own paths in life and hence, coercive states can deprive members of any level of realization.

The Democratic People's Republic of Korea is a prime example of how a state can prevent the development of personality, not only on an individual basis, but as a society as well. Seen by much of the world as a time machine to former days of Stalinist dominance, vibrancy and colour absent themselves from a land dominated by the hue of conformity. In buildings, in landscape, in literature. There is a standard that must be adhered to. An ideology that must be adhered to. North Korea would argue that this is "Juche"

Juche

"Juche" is the self-proclaimed 'political thesis' formed by Kim Il-Sung. Based on the principles of self-sufficiency, a strong military backbone and political independence, presenting Juche as a 'political thesis' masks the fact this Juche is an attempt by the regime to intellectualize and provide a philosophical backbone for how the regime organise society. North Korea has a strong military – if you count in terms of number of personnel on the books; however, a look at the resources and equipment the army has tells us that it is anything but strong. Yet, the main sticking point with Juche is not the military aspect, but the idea that North Korea is economically self-sufficient or has political independence.

Political independence entails, according to the late Kim Jong-Il, that "the people must have independence in thought and politics". However, this is not the case. Juche fails, and although may be seen as the state religion, is a façade. The state religion is the Kim Dynasty. The state religion is a cold-war mentality that the Americans are 'imperialist aggressors'. The state religion is that North Korea is superior to every other country in the world.

A cocktail of nationalism and isolation are taught to children from a young age. Conditioning and brainwashing. However, with the flow of information increasing into country through the border with China (South Korean and Chinese DVD's to name but a few sources of information), those who are not kept in line by the national ideology are kept in line by fear.

At each stage of a North Korean's personal development, there is a level of coercion by the state that prevents the free development of his personality.

Sadness

When travelling to North Korea, one looks out from the goldfish bowl of the tour bus and looks into the whites of the people's eyes. Smiles, joyfulness and innocence were found in only a few: children. Not yet realising the indoctrination they were experiencing, this is a time in a North Korean's life when they are able to enjoy developing their own personality in the same way that any child anywhere in the world does. Playing with friends, laughing, joking. But even at this stage; they are being moulded to how the state believes they should be: subservient. Take away the joyfulness of youth, and you can feel a sadness and dystopia that bears down upon the servants of the North Korean regime.

The sadness is multi-layered. Sadness that one doesn't have the basic economic means to provide for oneself; let alone one's family. Sadness that the social rights that are to be found naturally to many citizens of the world are not bestowed upon them by the system they are so unfortunate to be born into. Sadness that one isn't allowed to pursue his or her's own life, without coercion.

Hard Times

Charles Dickens wrote a book titled "Hard Times", detailing the utilitarian philosophy and it's role in Victorian education. Everything is to be done a set way, with logic and reason being the focal point of everything taught. Towards the end of the second book, one of the main characters, Louisa, breaks down in front of her father who had imposed a utilitarian education on her;

"How could you give me life, and take from me all the inappreciable things that raise it from the state of conscious death? Where are the graces of my soul? Where are the sentiments of my heart? What have you done, O father, what have you done, with the garden that should have bloomed once, in this great wilderness here... Yet, father, if I had been stone blind; if I had groped my way by my sense of touch, and had been free, while I knew the shapes and surfaces of things, to exercise my fancy somewhat, in regard to them; I should have been a million times wiser, happier, more loving, more contented, more innocent and human in all good respects, than I am with the eyes I have."[1]

---

[1] Dickens, Charles. *Hard Times.* Oxford: Oxford University Press, 2008.

The difference between the world Dickens' portrays and the North Korean world is that one is fictional, another reality. Whereas in Hard Times, Louisa's father had the best of intentions and was blinded by an ideology, the North Korean regime doesn't have the best of intentions for it's people, and is blinded by megalomania. However, if the North Korean people were free from coercion, were allowed a voice and a freedom that is not otherwise granted to them, I suspect many would feel exactly as Louisa did.

CLARA BLAMBERGER

ARTICLE 23
WOMEN WORK

"(1)Everyone has the right to work, to free choice of employment, to just and favourable conditions of work and to protection against unemployment. (2) Everyone, without any discrimination, has the right to equal pay for equal work. (3) Everyone who works has the right to just and favourable remuneration ensuring for himself and his family an existence worthy of human dignity, and supplemented, if necessary, by other means of social protection. (4) Everyone has the right to form and to join trade unions for the protection of his interests"

I've got the children to tend
The clothes to mend
The floor to mop
The food to shop
Then the chicken to fry
The baby to dry
I got company to feed
The garden to weed
I've got shirts to press
The tots to dress
The can to be cut
I gotta clean up this hut
Then see about the sick
And the cotton to pick.

Shine on me, sunshine
Rain on me, rain
Fall softly, dewdrops
And cool my brow again.

Storm, blow me from here
With your fiercest wind
Let me float across the sky
'Til I can rest again.

Fall gently, snowflakes
Cover me with white
Cold icy kisses and
Let me rest tonight.

Sun, rain, curving sky
Mountain, oceans, leaf and stone
Star shine, moon glow
You're all that I can call my own.

Women Work
by Maya Angelou

While this poem talks only of women and what is often the lack of choice they face in the work they do, its basic message is still simple, very general, and more than true: People often cannot choose their employment freely, cannot work under just and favourable conditions, and may not earn enough to live a life in dignity or are protected. Still, all over the world, people are forced into employment, and work under very hard conditions. Indeed, such conditions, and such forced employment are, as suggested by Angelou[1], often a result of societal values, and prescribed roles. They may also be a result of profound social inequality. This lack of freedom can therefore not be tackled on its own. It must be addressed alongside the other Articles of the Universal Declaration. To date, such a challenge has proven too great for us. Work, or a human life, it seems, is not much valued around the world. Unfortunately the reality remains an exact opposite of what is set out in Article 23 of the Universal Declaration of Human Rights.

[1] 'Woman Work', by Maya Angelou. Available at http://allpoetry.com/poem/8511443-Woman_Work-by-Maya_Angelou.

FREYA NOWELL

ARTICLE 24
POSITIVITY VS. PRODUCTIVITY: DEBATING THE MERITS OF A FOUR-DAY WEEK

"Everyone has the right to rest and leisure, including reasonable limitation of working hours and periodic holidays with pay."

Since this February, public sector workers in The Gambia have had the luxury of Fridays off. President Jammeh wants Gambians to devote more time to 'prayers, social activities and agriculture'.[1] Leisure time and holiday from work are elemental human rights as they are essential to a healthy and fulfilling lifestyle, as well as continued productivity in our jobs. So much of the world's population has no or little access to these rights, and yet working culture in the UK tends voluntarily towards excess beyond financial need and natural capacity. Why do we still live by a factory-line mentality that equates more time put in at work with higher output? Could we all do with a four-day week?

Attempts to prescribe the optimal work-life balance have always divided opinion. It is a question that takes into consideration both means of output efficiency and human wellbeing. Today, we take for granted the concept of a 'weekend' – a notion developed out of the religious observance of rest, with the traditional working days differing substantially between countries and cultures. The important role played by rest and recuperation in our lives is often belittled and our entitlement to it taken for granted. This stands in defiance of the historical progress governments, trade unions and individual companies have made in defending our right to leisure and paid holiday. In the United States, during the 'boom' of the 1920s, this sentiment was famously captured when car manufacturer Henry Ford closed his factories on both Saturday and Sunday, announcing 'the country is ready for the five-day week'.[2] In 1930, British economist John Maynard Keynes envisaged a 21st century of 15 hour weeks in which we had gained 'freedom from pressing economic cares' and chose to prioritise our leisure time.[3] Winston Churchill himself, not known for a lack of work ethic, predicted that the end of the Cold War would herald the era of 'a four-day week, then three days fun.'[4]

The right to rest and the limitation of working hours is part of the Universal Declaration for reasons more fundamental to the human condition than a desire for economic sensibility. The International Labour Organisation's (ILO) Conventions on working hours have been in place since 1919, aimed at ensuring 'high productivity while safeguarding workers' physical and mental health.'[5] The need for internationally accepted standards had long been pushed for by national trade unions and progressive industrialists, who feared competitive disadvantage but desired good working

---

[1] "Yahya Jammeh Gives Gambians An Extra Day Off." *BBC News: Africa.* 1 February 2013. Web. 25 April 2013. <http://www.bbc.co.uk/news/world-africa-21280766>.

[2] Price, Ian. "Four-day Working Week? Three Cheers!" *The Guardian.* 16 April 2011.Web. 25 April 2013. <http://www.guardian.co.uk/money/2011/apr/16/four-day-working-week>.

[3] Barford, Vanessa. "Should People be Off on Fridays?" *BBC News: Magazine.* 1 February 2013. Web. 25 April 2013. <http://www.bbc.co.uk/news/magazine-21242782>.

[4] Price, Ian. "Four-day Working Week? Three Cheers!" *The Guardian.* 16 April 2011.Web. 25 April 2013. <http://www.guardian.co.uk/money/2011/apr/16/four-day-working-week>.

[5] "Work Time" *International Labour Organization.* Web. 25 April 2013. <http://www.ilo.org/global/standards/subjects-covered-by-international-labour-standards/working-time/lang--en/>.

conditions for their employees. Today, ILO standards provide a framework for policies regulating weekly and daily hours of work, weekly rest and holidays with pay, as well as job-specific recommendations that cover night work and, more recently, part-time work. A universal right to humane labour conditions has only become more relevant given the global reach and competition of markets today. Even more so in light of advances in communications and technology that push workers beyond their physical and mental capacity.

As human beings, a direct relationship exists between our mental stimulation and levels of productivity. The nature of 21st century 'skilled' labour often makes it cognitively complex and highly demanding on brain function, in particular on the brain's pre-frontal cortex. At the same time, the way we work can be both long on hours and short on productivity when a deadly cocktail of caffeine and flip-chart consultation results in chaotic over-stimulation of the cortex, leaving us unable to focus. Psychologists and doctors often prescribe rest and recuperation to employees suffering from stress and attention deficit, understanding its importance for both long-term health and resilience at work. Studies have shown that, at 'positive', our brain functions improve every business outcome. In an ideal world, workers would experience job satisfaction that could account for any number of hours or hectic office environment. More often than not, we must make do with finding the respite we require to remain positive and productive in our time away from work. It is during leisure time that people are at their most creative and are most capable of problem solving. They are reflective, self-aware and innovative, indulging in their human desires for socialisation, satisfaction and discovery. Leisure activities are central to the development of local and national identities and culture. They enhance the living standards and social capital of all those involved in them, in particular of those most vulnerable in society. And yet, the majority of Britons are spending increasingly less time relaxing and socialising outside of work.

A growing 24/7 'on call' working culture spans the majority of the UK's economic sectors and poses a real threat to national standards for regulating time at work. Simultaneously though, technological advancement has opened up unique opportunities for re-evaluating methods of achieving a productive work-life balance. Teleworking, for instance, has become increasingly popular with the development of the internet and high-speed computing. A number of major companies including British Telecom and Dow Chemical have reported that teleworkers are 35% to 40% more productive.[6] Flexible working time policies encourage all employees to more effectively manage their work-life balance, but also inadvertently promote a number of other important human rights. They enable increased diversity in the labour force, by eliminating certain discriminations from the recruitment process, including race, religion, distance of commute and physical mobility. They can help to reconcile gender inequalities, both in the workplace and at home, as they allow for parents to more easily and equally balance their

[6] "Costs and Benefits." *Global Workplace Analysis.* Web. 25 April 2013. <http:// www.teleworkresearchnetwork.com/resources/costs-benefits>.

commitments to their careers with family responsibilities.

If a healthy, more flexible work-life balance is not being struck by the majority of British workers, perhaps passing legislation to reduce or redistribute our working hours would suit us just as well as the Gambian public sector. A YouGov poll carried out in February found that 72% of employed Britons were in fact in favour of a four-day week.[7] In 2010, a study by the UK-based New Economics Foundation forecast a major shift towards a shorter working week, identifying 21 hours as the optimum weekly workload.[8] The report found strong environmental, economic and social arguments for such a policy, which would allow people to live more sustainably, 'as active and fulfilled citizens'. Strong government policy on the issue could also help deplete the widening earnings gap that has only furthered restrictions on social mobility and incentives to put in longer hours, since the rewards for doing so are considerable. A number of states in America have experimented with the option of a four-day week, whilst in the Netherlands, one in three men employed today either works part-time or 40 hours in four days.[9] Here in the UK, as elsewhere, there are already a number of professions with a long history of working shorter weeks of longer shifts, journalists being among them.

Whilst employed Britons are overworking themselves despite highly increased living standards, Keynes' projection of freedom from material concerns has sadly not come to pass for the majority of the world's population. World Bank figures put nearly 1.3 billion people living below the extreme poverty line, with an income of US $1.25 or less a day.[10] The ILO's 2005 report on working standards found that, over the last twenty years, normal working hours had either remained the same or increased in over one hundred countries.[11] A universal five-day week is a distant reality in this respect, let alone a four-day one. It is a sad reality that almost all workers in the UK enjoy a right to regulated rest, leisure and paid holiday without full respect for its multi-faceted importance. Following the lead of The Gambia and questioning the distribution of our traditional working hours would be a good step towards acknowledging the place of human fulfilment in our working and non-working lives.

---

[7] "Brits Want 4 Day Week." *YouGov.* Web. 28 February 2013.<http://yougov.co.uk/news/2013/02/28/brits-want-4-day-week/>.

[8] Boyle, David. "Keynes and the Treasury." *New Economics.* 24 June 2010. Web. 25 April 2013. <http://www.neweconomics.org/blog%20?page=116&iframe=true&width=100%25&height=100%25>.

[9] Barford, Vanessa. "Should People be Off on Fridays?" *BBC News: Magazine.* 1 February 2013. Web. 25 April 2013. <http://www.bbc.co.uk/news/magazine-21242782>.

[10] "Poverty Overview." *World Bank.* Web. 25 April 2013. <http://www.worldbank.org/en/topic/poverty/overview>.

[11] *Hours of Work: From Fixed to Flexible?* (Rep) International Labour Organization. Web. 25 April 2013. <http://www.ilo.org/public/english/standards/relm/ilc/ilc93/pdf/rep-iii-1b.pdf>.

STEPHANIE DAVID

ARTICLE 25
ON FEMALE GENITAL MUTILATION

"(1) Everyone has the right to a standard of living adequate for the health and well-being of himself and of his family, including food, clothing, housing and medical care and necessary social services, and the right to security in the event of unemployment, sickness, disability, widowhood, old age or other lack of livelihood in circumstances beyond his control.
(2) Motherhood and childhood are entitled to special care and assistance. All children, whether born in or out of wedlock, shall enjoy the same social protection."

So much could be said in relation to this Article, especially under our current Government's austerity measures that have cut basic benefits and social welfare support.[1] I intend to consider a specific case that relates to Article 25, namely Female Genital Mutilation (FGM), and how the UK Government is seeking to uphold Article 25 in relation this practise. I will commend recent Government efforts to address FGM overseas, however I will question whether criminalizing the practise in the UK is the best way of protecting young girls and women at risk in this country.

FGM, otherwise known as Female Genital Cutting and Female Circumcision, can involve partial or total removal of the clitoris, or the sealing of the vaginal opening.[2] Girls and women who have undergone FGM often suffer from infections, urine retention and fatal haemorrhaging; damage to their reproductive systems; and serious complications in childbirth.[3] According to UK Government sources, the practise affects around 140 million women and girls around the world, with about 95% of cases in Africa.[4] In the UK, it is estimated that 20-24,000 girls are at risk and 66,000 women are living with the consequences of FGM.[5]

International consensus is clearly moving against this abhorrent practise. On December 20, 2012, the United Nations General Assembly unanimously passed a

---

[1] The current Coalition government's policies may violate many individuals' Article 25 rights. The so-called 'bedroom tax' may lead to homelessness as housing benefit will be cut according to whether families have a spare room. The social protection of children is being eroded by the changes in child benefit. Finally, changes in legal aid with the coming into force of the Legal Aid, Sentencing and Punishment of Offenders Act will mean that individuals will no longer have legal support to contest some employment and education decisions or in divorce or custody battles. Moreover, these measures will disproportionately affect the 'very poorest and the most disadvantaged' according to Lord Bach. This means that these policies may not only violate the basic rights outlined in Article 25 of the UDHR, but also violate non-discrimination principles as embodied in Article 2 of the UDHR.

[2] Firmin, Carlene. "Female Genital Mutilation: The UK Must Act Now." *The Guardian.* 26 March 2013. Web. 25 April 2013.<http://www.guardian.co.uk/society/2013/mar/26/female-genital-mutilation-preventive-approach>.

[3] Ibid

[4] United Kingdom. Department for International Development. *A Time For Change: Ending Female Genital Mutilation.* 22 March 2013. Web. 26 March 2013. <https://www.gov.uk/government/case-studies/a-time-for-change-ending-female-genital-mutilation>.

[5] Firmin, Carlene. "Female Genital Mutilation: The UK Must Act Now." *The Guardian.* 26 March 2013. Web. 25 April 2013.<http://www.guardian.co.uk/society/2013/mar/26/female-genital-mutilation-preventive-approach>.

resolution banning the practice.[6] The UK has taken a commendable leading role in building this emerging consensus to combat the practice. At the 57th session of the Commission on the Status of Women, Lynne Featherstone, the Minister for International Development, committed an impressive £35 million to eradicating the practise worldwide, which will be spent on research into how to end the practise and community-based initiatives to address and ultimately end FGM.[7]

However, the focus of the UK policy seems to be rather on combating the practise overseas and changing the attitudes abroad. What about the girls who 'disappear' from schools all over the UK to undergo the practise? The UK currently criminalises FGM under the Female Genital Mutilation Act 2003, which came into effect in March 2004.[8] However, not one prosecution has been brought under the Act to date.[9] This fact clearly demonstrates that the UK Government is not taking the correct approach in the UK to address the practise. Criminalising family members, who are often the perpetrators of this culturally entrenched practise, is unlikely to yield positive results. Admittedly, the Government is seeking to encourage midwives to broach the subject with potential victims.[10] However, these combined approaches are not adequate for addressing the roots of the problem as a deeply culturally entrenched and private affair. Rather, the Government should focus on promoting cultural and attitudinal change. As John Hendra, UN Women Assistant-Secretary General and Deputy Executive Director suggested 'practical actions [of] bringing perpetrators to justice,' must be 'backed up with services for victims, engaging key influencers and supporting community-based activities to change social norms.'[11]

Therefore, in order to ensure that the UK adequately protects the Article 25 rights of girls and women at risk in the UK, she should take a much more holistic approach to addressing the practise. Donating vast sums of money to overseas projects, however laudable, will not suffice to fulfil the UK's obligations under the UDHR to girls and women in this country.

---

[6] UN Women, "United Nations Bans Female Genital Mutilation." *UN Nations.* 20 December 2012. Web. 26 March 2013. <http://www.unwomen.org/2012/12/united-nations-bans-female-genital-mutilation/>.

[7] Ford, Liz. "UK Funds Aim to End Female Genital Mutilation 'in a Generation'." *The Guardian.* 6 March 2013. Web. 26 March 2013. <http://www.guardian.co.uk/global-development/2013/mar/06/uk-funds-female-genital-mutilation-generation>.

[8] United Kingdom. Home Office. *Policy: Ending Violence Against Women and Girls in the UK.* Web. 26 March 2013. <https://www.gov.uk/government/policies/ending-violence-against-women-and-girls-in-the-uk>.

[9] United Kingdom. Hansard, Commons Debates: *Justice: Female Genital Mutilation: Prosecutions.* 3 November 2010. Web. 26 March 2013. <http://www.publications.parliament.uk/pa/cm201011/cmhansrd/cm101103/text/101103w0002.htm>.

[10] "Midwife 'Role' as NHS Targets Female Genital Mutilation." *BBC News: UK.* 2 February 2013. Web. 26 March 2013. <http://www.bbc.co.uk/news/uk-21306861>.

[11] UN Women, "United Nations Bans Female Genital Mutilation." *UN Nations.* 20 December 2012. Web. 26 March 2013. <http://www.unwomen.org/2012/12/united-nations-bans-female-genital-mutilation/>.

Rachel Williams

Article 26
Malala

"(1) Everyone has the right to education. Education shall be free, at least in the elementary and fundamental stages. Elementary education shall be compulsory. Technical and professional education shall be made generally available and higher education shall be equally accessible to all on the basis of merit.
(2) Education shall be directed to the full development of the human personality and to the strengthening of respect for human rights and fundamental freedoms. It shall promote understanding, tolerance and friendship among all nations, racial or religious groups, and shall further the activities of the United Nations for the maintenance of peace.
(3) Parents have a prior right to choose the kind of education that shall be given to their children."

"I don't mind if I have to sit on the floor at school. All I want is education. And I am afraid of no-one."

ELIZABETH STOUT

ARTICLE 27
ON INTELLECTUAL PROPERTY RIGHTS

"(1) Everyone has the right freely to participate in the cultural life of the community, to enjoy the arts and to share in scientific advancement and its benefits.
(2) Everyone has the right to the protection of the moral and material interests resulting from any scientific, literary or artistic production of which he is the author."

The protection of moral and materials interests resulting from any scientific, literary or artistic production is today a very different matter than it was in 1948, when the Universal Declaration of Human Rights was authored. In a digital era, the protection of such interests becomes increasingly difficult, and the necessity of this protection becomes open to question. It is in Article 27, perhaps above any other Article, that the relevance of the Universal Declaration to modern society is called into question. However, as can be inferred from other Articles of the UDHR, the achievements of these rights, and indeed the universal recognition of these rights remains highly volatile. For the Articles to be brought into question seems to greatly decrease the likelihood of countries working towards them. Indeed, if the UDHR cannot be said to apply to the most developed countries, which often pressure less developed countries to improve their human rights record, how can this pressure legitimately continue? Although the non-binding UDHR is by no means the only measure of countries human rights records, meaning that an increasing scepticism towards it may not ostensibly diminish the potential for the fulfillment of human rights, it is however the only human rights agreement that is 'Universal.' In this sense, it remains the most effective standard by which to measure human rights by. It has already been brought into question whether countries such as the UK and the US are acting towards the fulfillment of the UDHR. Where yet another Article is not abided by, the achievement of universal human rights may become even more difficult.

How can such a situation be avoided? Firstly, it is necessary to observe the degree to which these rights have become unattainable in a digital age. And secondly, it is necessary to determine whether such a change may compromise the UDHR's ability to be universal across both time and space.

It is important to recognise the differences that may exist between 'scientific, literary or artistic production', and the capacity for these to be both morally and materially protected. To first address the moral and material protection of scientific productions, we note that in an industry which is so heavily privatized, scientific productions are perhaps less under threat in a digital age than literary or artistic productions. It is, perhaps, easier to share or recreate a literary or artistic production than it is a scientific one, with access to material being a key preventative factor. It may seem then that the material interests of those who have authored scientific productions may not be open to question. However, two factors must be taken into account. Firstly, that not all scientific productions may be regarded in the same way, and thus that which applies to one may not apply to others. And secondly, the protection of moral interests must be questioned. And it is here we meet a case in which the protection of material interests of scientific production may be brought into direct opposition with protection of moral interests. In his recent book *Bad Pharma*,

Ben Goldacre reveals to us a case in which a pharmaceuticals company developed a drug intended to treat children suffering from depression. Goldacre revealed that although the drug was found to be ineffective during trials, the need to protect the material interests of its authors was so great that the drug was put into production anyway, and the trial results altered, despite its inability to perform its function.[1] This would appear unquestionably immoral. The protection of that which a person has created may be seen to be necessarily moral as they are entitled to this protection from the fact that their own labour created it, that their own personality was put into it, and that it allows a person to "carve out an area of individual dominion."[2] Thus it would seem that to the extent that these factors are protected, the actions of this company were moral. They acted to preserve their own ability, and incentive, to continue to produce. Article 27 provides only for the moral interests of the creator.

What must be questioned here, however, is to whose moral interests such actions are to the detriment to. To those in receipt of the drug, it may adversely impact upon their mental and physical interests. And to those in purchase of the drug may, their material interests may be adversely affected. Thus the only group whose morality is in fact in question is those who put the drug into production despite knowledge of its inutility. Their moral interests may be the only ones adversely affected, as it is their morals which will suffer as a result of their actions. Financial incentive thus allows for and indeed creates such immorality. Thus we observe that with regard to some scientific production, ensuring the protection of both moral and material interests proves an often unattainable goal. Yet as stated above, there are few who would regard this activity as moral. However, we note that Article 27 also states the need to protect the moral interests of the author. If the moral interests of the author pertain to his or her own morality, here we see a failure to protect this. Thus it would appear that in seeking to protect their own material interests, producers may sacrifice their own moral interests, and in doing so cause a detriment to others. The sustainability of the protection of material production must therefore be questioned.

This would then bring us to the question of literary and artistic production. As stated above, in a digital era, such rights become increasingly difficult to protect. Literary production can be copied and illegally downloaded. 'Artistic production' can be seen as a term applying to all forms of arts, within which 'mashups'[3] may be made of musical creations, as well as recordings made without the payment of royalties. Television and film may be pirated. And these may all be carried out by otherwise law-abiding citizens, and may be so widespread that any form of punishment or even acknowledgement of the crime remains unlikely. Thus a new question is raised. Does the maintenance of Article 27 require a violation of Article 19, that people may 'receive and impart information and ideas through any media and regardless of frontiers'?

It was certainly not the intent of the authors of the Universal Declaration that this Declaration be amended due to a perceived unfeasibility of its acheivement. It may be

---

[1] Goldacre, Ben. "Bad Pharma: How Drug Companies Mislead Doctors and Harm Patients." 2012. London: Fourth Estate. pp. 56-59.

[2] Spence, Michael. "The Justification of Intellectual Property." *Intellectual Property,* 2007. Oxford: Oxford University Press. pp 46 - 52.

[3] Constanides, Panos. "The Development and Consequences of New Information Infrastructures: The Case of Mashup Platforms." *Media, Culture and Society.* 34.5 (2012): 606-622.

argued that such cases as have been outlined above are extreme, and the protection of intellectual property rights is necessary and moral in the majority of cases. It may be argued that the alteration of one Article of the UDHR may lead to a slippery slope on which human rights are sacrificed, one by one, to fit with the developments of the modern era. Such arguments carry more than an element of truth.

Thus we have reached an impasse. It would seem that at present, Article 27 allows a great scope for violation in not pertaining to the realities of modern society, and in this it is becoming increasingly unlikely to be achieved. We have also seen the damage that can be done by the upholding of this right. But at present we are unaware of the damage that may be done to society in the absence of intellectual property rights, as a result of a reduction in incentive. And we are also unaware of the damage it would do to the inviolability of the UDHR to make an amendment.

Herein lies a situation in which society is changing so rapidly that we cannot yet know the best course of action to be taken. All that can be said is this: it is perhaps unreasonable to expect a Declaration made in 1948 to pertain directly to modern society. However, the flaws in Article 27 have been noted. The term of 'material and moral interests' is perhaps one open to interpretations other than those outlined above. What we can hope is that, in light of the issues raised, Article 27 will be applied in such a way to apply contextually, and in such a way that will prevent a detriment to others.

JAMIE PELLING

ARTICLE 28
THE NECESSITY OF THE ARMS TRADE TREATY

"Everyone is entitled to a social and international order in which the rights and freedoms set forth in this Declaration can be fully realized."

History was made in March, when the United Nations met again to discuss a new Arms Trade Treaty. Following unsuccessful, and ultimately disappointing negotiations last July, the international community formed the first treaty regulating the arms trade. The treaty aims to inhibit the ability of governments around the world to sell arms to unstable regimes, militia, or various other non-state actors. The treaty did not need to be, nor is it a revolutionary act banning the trading of all arms, it is merely a first step. This first step has been a long time in coming and the arms trade has been implicated in some of the worst human rights atrocities since the Second World War. Human rights and the arms trade are inextricably linked and if the UN is to live up to its reputation as outlined in Article 28 of the Universal Declaration on Human Rights, then it must take action to reduce the prevalence of the international arms trade. The treaty must constitute this action.

The case study used by Amnesty International when examining the link between the arms trade and Human Rights violations is that of the Democratic Republic of Congo.[1] An AK-47 is, according to Amnesty's report, seen as a 'credit card' in the war-torn Eastern areas of the country, enabling members of the Congolese military to exchange their government-issued weapon for substantial material gain. It is a well-documented process by which these death-dealing small arms fall into the hands of rebels. Atrocities have been committed on both sides, largely with weapons imported from countries including, China, France, South Africa, and that fine purveyor of arms, the USA. Indeed, these suppliers are well aware of the problems in the DRC, yet continue to supply the military, and thus the rebels with arms, fuelling a deplorable civil war for the profit of their own economies. Another troubling example is that of the Sudan.[2] Here, the supply of arms far outnumbered the supply of soldiers, so much so that the use of children in warfare became the norm. A brutal civil conflict which lasted 22 years has left an indelible mark on modern Sudan; there are still thousands in refugee camps vulnerable and unable to return home. Clearly the arms trade is exacerbating civil and international conflicts around the world and the UN has a duty to regulate, if not put an end to, its existence.

The connection between the flow of small arms and human rights abuse is evident; 60% of all violations involve small arms. For every person on the earth there are two bullets produced and $1,738 billion spent on arms each year.[3] Just $7 billion is spent on

[1] "An AK-47 - Often The 'Credit Card' For FARDC Soldiers." *Amnesty International.* Web. 25 April 2013. <http://www2.amnesty.org.uk/blogs/press-release-me-let-me-go/ak-47-often-credit-card-fardc-soldiers>.

[2] "Former Sudan Child Soldier Emmanuel Jal to Speak Out on Global Arms Trade Treaty with Amnesty International Media Tour March 5-7 in New York and Washington, D.C." *Amnesty International USA.* 25 February 2013. Web. 25 April 2013. <http://www.amnestyusa.org/news/press-releases/former-sudan-child-soldier-emmanuel-jal-to-speak-out-on-global-arms-trade-treaty-with-amnesty-intern>.

[3] Naidoo, Kumi. "Two Bullets per Person: The Trillion Dollar Military Spending Club." Web log post. 17 April 2012. Web. 25 April 2013. <http://www.greenpeace.org/international/en/news/Blogs/makingwaves/two-bullets-per-person-the-trillion-dollar-mi/blog/40000/>.

peacekeeping.[4] These statistics are shocking, there are more arms produced each year and they remain in circulation for decades. Russian Kalashnikov rifles from the 1950s are still in use around the world, an agreement is necessary in order to, as one Oxfam spokesperson put it, turn off the taps and enable us to drain the bath.[5] The first draft released of the ATT certainly reduced the gushing taps to a dribble, but there were loopholes which must be shut. Ammunition was not yet included in the draft treaty, an essential provision which can stop civil conflict immediately. In Mali, before the latest Islamist insurgency, the opposing sides on the civil war had been brought to the negotiating table because the rebels had run out of ammunition. This loophole was closed in the final draft. However, there remain issues concerning definitions: what defines a failed state; what defines a civil war; what even defines Human Rights abuse.

There may still be impediments to its success. While almost every nation fell behind the plan to write a treaty during the March 2013 talks, there were abstentions: Iran, Syria, and North Korea. While small in number, such abstentions prevented the strengthening of the treaty through its adoption by consensus. Even those who stood in favour initially appeared to have radically differing aims. Russia, which profits a great deal from the open trading of arms, had a radically different agenda to Mexico, whose focus is on limiting the arms supply to its infamous drug barons. Article 28 of the UDHR states that 'Everyone is entitled to a social and international order in which the rights and freedoms set forth in this Declaration can be fully realized'. Had March passed, like July before it, without a treaty, the UN would have failed to uphold this article. However, the UN has achieved what had become a necessity, for global Human Rights, and for the UN's image as its protector. The international community may stand hopeful, as another step towards the achievement of our rights has been fulfilled.

---

[4] "Peacekeeping Budgets and Personnel Soar to New Heights." *Worldwatch Institute.* Web. 25 April 2013. <http://www.worldwatch.org/node/5466>.

[5] "Shattered Lives: The Case For Tough International Arms Control." *Control Arms.* Web. 25 April 2013. <http://controlarms.org/wordpress/wp-content/uploads/2011/02/Shattered-lives-the-case-for-tough-international-arms-control.pdf> .

Michael Pearson

Article 29
A Technological Underground

"(1) Everyone has duties to the community in which alone the free and full development of his personality is possible. (2) In the exercise of his rights and freedoms, everyone shall be subject only to such limitations as are determined by law solely for the purpose of securing due recognition and respect for the rights and freedoms of others and of meeting the just requirements of morality, public order and the general welfare in a democratic society. (3) These rights and freedoms may in no case be exercised contrary to the purposes and principles of the United Nations."

Imagine a country where you have no access to the Internet. Imagine a country where you are forbidden from spreading information about the outside world. Imagine a country that uses surveillance to monitor your phone calls to ensure you are not being politically subversive. No Google, Facebook, YouTube or Twitter. Imagine a country where the flows of information are restricted by the state, and freedom of expression is an alien concept. There's no need to imagine; North Korea is this place.

Technology plays a key role in empowering people politically, the most effective of which is the way in which Internet and telecommunications enables the flow of information. Technology can empower people in the political process in many ways, but the flow of information brought by the Internet and telecommunications brings empowers the people the most.

The freedom to establish networks of communications and share thoughts and opinions without recrimination lies at the heart of every democratic society.

For decades, the North Korean state has understood the importance of flows of information. Media is state-controlled and communications are monitored. Whilst the Arab world uses Twitter as a vehicle to advance political mobilization, the regime will feel vindicated in ensuring technology's role is to advance and stabilize the party machine.

However, the landscape in North Korea has been changing recently. Eager to not be seen to be stalling in a Stalinist time vacuum, they have allowed foreigners in the country to make international phone calls and access mobile internet, aimed at encouraging foreign investment.[1] [Since the time of writing, they have cut the service after only a month.[2]] However, the real change is bottom-up. South Korean DVDs flood the markets from illegal channels in China. Foreign radio broadcasts populate living rooms and bedrooms across the Hermit kingdom. A survey of 1,486 defectors in 2011 found that the most common methods of outside information are CDs and DVDs (37.2 per cent), verbal communication (22.4 per cent) and foreign radio broadcasts (14.1 per cent).[3]

Although radio and DVDs may appear outdated by Western standards of on-

---

[1] Park, Seong Guk. "Koryolink Mobile Internet Launched." *Daily NK.* 26 February 2013. Web. 25 April 2013. <http://www.dailynk.com/english/read.php?cataId=nk00100&num=10345>.

[2] Cho, Jong Ik. "Tourist Internet Cut After a Month." *Daily NK.* 29 March 2013. Web. 25 April 2013. <http://www.dailynk.com/english/read.php?cataId=nk00100&num=10448>.

[3] Seo, Yoon Hwan. "Whither Information Freedom in 'Reforming' NK?" *Daily NK.* 13 September 2013. Web. 25 April 2013. <http://www.dailynk.com/english/read.php?cataId=nk03600&num=9787>.

demand radio, podcasts, Netflix and LoveFilm, these technological forms provide key information that allow people to compare their lives with that of those across the border and beyond. South Korean dramas have gained underground popularity as perceptions of the outside world. In the same survey of defectors, when asked the effect of outside information, the most common effects were "admiration for foreign societies" (44 per cent) and "desire to defect" (33 per cent).

It's not only in media consumption that technology is helping to drive flows of information. The security forces have cracked down on the use of mobile phones to make calls abroad. Brought into China through smugglers, people use their mobiles by riding fast on bicycles or walking at a pace down the street to avoid detection by the authorities.

They use Chinese mobiles as the North Korean mobile system is monitored by the state. Orascom, an Egyptian telecommunications company with operations in Egypt, Algeria and Tunisia ventured to the DPRK to set up a mobile phone network in a society that knows not the meaning of freedom of speech.

As a result, the Orascom supported network has over 1 million users and is proving to be extremely profitable for the country. Angel Dobardziev of Ovum noted that the earnings before tax margin of an "emerging market is generally recorded at 30-35 per cent, but in North Korea we know it to be around 64 per cent". [4] Because of this, he argues that Orascom "faithfully tows the line on what the regime wants".

Besides, the regime has no incentive to open up channels of communications. Priority number one post-Kim Jong-Il is to stabilize the regime under Kim Jong-Un and ensure no underlying political thought pervades society; just blind worship of the Kims.

However, blocking these flows can only happen for so long. "Illegal" technological means of accessing information are on the up and show no sign of abating. Having said this, the majority of the mobile phones in use are in the show-city Pyongyang in the possession of the elite, with rural communities being left behind.

On visiting North Korea last year, I went to the Grand People's Study House in Pyongyang, the country's largest library. Gathering around a computer, we attempted to find books on the library's database. When we asked if they had any books on The Holocaust, our guide replied, "Is that a famous English book?"

This highlighted that although information is being spread to a greater extent (one of our guides had even heard of the Royal Wedding), there is still a long way to go.

Politically subversive behaviour in North Korea is still dangerous. Unless the state changes its policies, any political change in the country will be driven by technology bought or accessed through illegal methods. Bottom-up rather than top-down, technology may well empower the people to call for change. Knowledge is power; and the North Korean regime knows it.

---

[4] Green, Chris. "2% of North Koreans Now Use Orascom." *Daily NK.* 19 April 2011. Web. 25 April 2013. <http://www.dailynk.com/english/read.php?cataId=nk00100&num=7589>.

JADE JACKMAN

ARTICLE 30
NOT INCLUDING THE DEATH PENALTY

"Nothing in this Declaration may be interpreted as implying for any State, group or person any right to engage in any activity or to perform any act aimed at the destruction of any of the rights and freedoms set forth herein."

The Universal Declaration of Human Rights does not forbid the death penalty. Article 30 neatly rounds up the declaration through the statement, 'nothing in this declaration may be interpreted as implying any state, group or person any right to engage in any activity or to perform any act aimed at the destruction if any rights and freedoms set forth herein.' As the death penalty is not explicitly prohibited it can still be used even though it is implicitly against the terms of Article 3 and 5. This incongruence raises questions about society's portrayal of criminals. Criminals who commit merciless acts of violence are often referred to as 'monsters' or, perhaps, 'sadistic animals'. In using such language, not only do we obscure the stark reality of their crimes but we also protect our species from 'pollution' by disassociating humanity with these depraved criminals.

In order to satisfy our somewhat morbid fascination with America's executions, Sir Trevor McDonald recently journeyed to Indiana's maximum-security state prison.[1] One journalist commented that he attempted to take a more 'objective' tone when relaying back his findings. This may have been his intention, but instead he crossed the fine line between objectivity and dispassion. One of the prisoners, a Ronald L. Sanford, was convicted of a double homicide at the tender age of thirteen. At 13, he was condemned to 170 years of imprisonment. McDonald pauses, and then comments, 'it's a long time when you come in at the age of 13'.

In combination with other statements, such as 'it's [the prison] a pretty isolating place', make it hard to discern whether this remark says more about the ITV's perception of the intellectual limitations of their viewers or the lack of compassion shown towards prisoners in order to condone such treatment. Of course, there are merits in providing such a scientific analysis but such a detached attitude prevents us from challenging our own views on the death penalty. Furthermore, it is this emotionless and disengaged attitude that allows for the ambiguity between Articles 3, 5 and 30.

As much as we may try and deny it, drug lords and paedophiles are not demonic forces that emerge at night to devour their prey. They are humans, rather like you and I. This sentiment is encapsulated in Werner Herzog's rather controversial series revolving around death row.[2] It is undeniable that he is an advocate for prison reform in America, nevertheless his documentaries provoke his audience into questioning whether we can really take any crime at face value.

Herzog encounters James Barnes. Barnes originally had been given 8 years in prison, until he confessed to another brutal murder for which he was given the

---

[1] McDonald, Sir Trevor. *Inside Death Row With Trevor McDonald*. ITV. 17 January 2013 and 24 January 2013. Television.

[2] Herzog, Werner. *Death Row*. Channel 4. 22 March 2012, 29 March 2013 and Thursday 5 April 2013. Television.

death sentence. His murders were cold-hearted and pre-meditated. Herzog provides his viewers with a full account of how Barnes stripped naked then hid waiting in order to rape and murder his victim. In an attempt to cover up his guilt, he set the woman's bed alight and fled the scene. Many among us will believe that the perpetrator of such an atrocity deserves chemical castration and that through his own cruelty that he has destroyed his right to life. Yet, Herzog manages to show that there is still something decidedly human lurking under the surface of Barnes' merciless crimes. The 'deformity' of his mind is not redeemed but is instead humanised by Herzog's inclusion of his appreciation of the natural world. Naturally, criminals deserve to be punished for the crimes that they commit and such actions should be deemed as inexcusable. However, hiding these people behind the metaphor of 'monster' only gives rise to confusion, as demonstrated by the conflict between Article 30 and 3 and 5. A monster is, of course, not a person.

The reality of the situation is when an individual commits an act so heinous we desire to transform them into a sub-human or an anomaly of society. We cannot stand such individuals being humanised because we may recognise their traits in ourselves; the more such an individual is humanised the more problematic an outlook of this nature becomes. The realisation that we cannot relegate these people to a sub-stratum of society is a difficult one to grasp and is not made easier by the fact that this group of people can legally have their lives terminated. Every human has a right to liberty, except those who have forsaken their humanity and so become animals.

Unsurprisingly, Herzog's 'attempt to humanize his subjects' has been a common critique of his work. However, it is clear that he does not attempt to provide these criminals with features that they lack. Each and every one of them is already human, we just need to be reminded of that.

BIBLIOGRAPHY

ARTICLE 1

Beijing Platform for Action. Rep. United Nations Documents, September 1995. Web. 8 April 2013. <http://www.un-documents.net/bpa-4-b.htm> accessed 8/4/2013.

Bowcott, Owen. "Afghanistan Worst Place in World for Women, but India in Top Five." *The Guardian,* 15 June 2011. Web. 8 April 2013. <http://www.guardian.co.uk/world/2011/jun/15/worst-place-women-afghanistan-india> accessed 8/4/2013.

Burke, Jason. "Delhi Gang-Rape Accused Face Rape and Murder Charges." *The Guardian,* 3 January 2013. Web. 8 April 2013. <http://www.guardian.co.uk/world/2013/jan/03/delhi-gang-rape-accused-murder-charges>.

Gender Pay Gap Statistics. Rep. European Commission, March 2013. Web. 8 April 2013. <http://epp.eurostat.ec.europa.eu/statistics_explained/index.php/Gender_pay_gap_statistics>.

Ghosh, Palash R. "Selective Abortion Of Female Fetuses In India Creating Gender Imbalance Crisis." *International Business Times*, 19 September 2012. Web. 8 April 2013. <http://www.ibtimes.com/selective-abortion-female-fetuses-india-creating-gender-imbalance-crisis-793298>.

India. Ministry of Home Affairs. National Crime Records Bureau. *Crime in India 2011.* 28 June 2012. Web. 8 April 2013. <http://ncrb.nic.in/CD-CII2011/cii-2011/Chapter%205.pdf>.

"India Ranked 'Worst' G-20 Country to be a Woman; Canada Declared the Best." *International Business Times: Traveller.* Web. 8 April 2013. <http://www.ibtimes.co.in/articles/352199/20120614/india-worst-country-woman-canada-best-saudi.htm>.

Inequalities and Multiple Discrimination in Access to Healthcare. Rep. European Union Agency for Fundamental Rights. 2011. Web. 11 April 2013. <http://fra.europa.eu/sites/default/files/fra_uploads/1421-Multiple-discrimination_Factsheet_EN.pdf>.

"International Women's Day 2012: Women's Representation in Politics." *The Guardian,* March 2012. Web. 8 April 2013. <http://www.guardian.co.uk/news/datablog/2012/mar/07/women-representation-in-politics-worldwide>.

Khazan, Olga "How India's rape name-and-shame database could backfire." *The Washington Post*, 28 December 2012. Web. 8 April 2013. <http://www.washingtonpost.com/blogs/worldviews/wp/2012/12/28/how-indias-rape-name-and-shame-database-could-backfire/>.

"Millions of female foetuses aborted in India." *The Telegraph*, 24 May 2011. Web. 8 April 2013. <http://www.telegraph.co.uk/news/worldnews/asia/india/8532190/Millions-of-female-foetuses-aborted-in-India.html>.

Morales, Zia. "Empowering Women is Smart Economics." Web log post. *The World Bank,* 15 October 2012. Web. 11 April 2013. <http://blogs.worldbank.org/psd/empowering-women-is-smart-economics>.

Pidd, Helen. "Why is India so Bad for Women." *The Guardian,* 23 July 2012. Web. 8 April 2013. <http://www.guardian.co.uk/world/2012/jul/23/why-india-bad-for-women>.

"Rape and Murder in Delhi." *The Economist,* 5 January 2013. Web. 8 April 2013. <http://www.economist.com/news/leaders/21569031-horrible-attack-could-prove-turning-point-indias-women-rape-and-murder-delhi>.

Smith-Spark, Laura. "How Did Rape Become a Weapon of War?" *BBC News.* Web. 8 April 2013. <http://news.bbc.co.uk/1/hi/4078677.stm>

Women and Drug Abuse: The Problem in India. Rep. United Nations International Drug Control Program and Ministry of Social Justice and Empowerment, 6 May 2003. Web. 8 April 2013. <https://www.unodc.org/pdf/india/publications/women_Book 6 5 03/09_statusofwomeninindia.pdf>

"Women and Poverty" *Global Poverty Info Bank.* Web. 8 April 2013. <http://www.globalpovertyproject.com/infobank/women>.

Article 4

International Labour Organization. *21 Million People Are Now Victims of Forced Labour, ILO Says.* 1 June 2012. Web. 24 April 2013. <http://www.ilo.org/global/about-the-ilo/newsroom/news/WCMS_181961/lang--en/index.htm>.

"Slavery: A 21st Century Evil." 25 November 2011. Television. Web. 20 March 2013.<http://www.aljazeera.com/programmes/slaverya21stcenturyevil/>.

Article 5

Babar Ahmad and others v. The United Kingdom, 24027/07, Council of Europe: ECHR 609, 10 April 2012.

Balabou Mutombo v. Switzerland, CAT/C/12/D/013/1993, UN Committe Against Torture, 27 April 1994.

C. v. Australia, CCPR/C/76/D/900/1999, UN Human Rights Committe, 13 November 2002

Campbell, Duncan. "US Interrogators Turn to 'Torture Lite'." 25 July 2003. Web. 12 April 2013. <http://www.guardian.co.uk/world/2003/jan/25/usa.alqaida>.

Chahal v. The United Kingdom, 70/1995/576/662. Council of Europe: European Court of Human Rights, 15 November 1996.

Charles Chitat Ng v. Canada, CCPR/C/49/D/469/1991, UN Human Rights Committee, 7 January 1994.

D. v. The United Kingdom, 146/1996/767/964, Council of Europe: ECHR, 2 May 1997.

Dershowitz, Alan. "Tortured Reasoning," *International Human Rights in Context: Law, Politics, Morals*. Ed. Henry J. Steiner, Ryan Goodman and Philip Alston, 3rd ed. Oxford: Oxford University Press, 2008. 250.

"Europe Must Halt Unreliable 'Diplomatic Assurances' That Risk Torture." *Amnesty International.* 12 April 2010. Web. 15 April 2013. <http://www.amnesty.org/en/news-and-updates/report/europe-must-halt-unreliable-diplomatic-assurances-risk-torture-2010-04-12>.

Joseph, Sarah, Jenny Schultz and Melissa Castan, *The International Covenant on Civil and Political Rights: Cases, Commentary and Materials*. Oxford: Oxford Univerysity Press, 2000.

Judd, Terri. "Abu Qatada Stays in UK: Theresa May Under Pressure After Another Judicial Rebuff." *The Independent.* 27 March 2013. Web. 16 April 2013. <http://www.independent.co.uk/news/uk/home-news/abu-qatada-stays-in-uk-theresa-may-under-pressure-after-another-juducial-rebuff-8550895.html>.

N. v. The United Kingdom, 26565/05, Council of Europe: ECHR 453, 27 May 2008.

"Non-refoulement." United Nations Educational, Scientific and Cultural Organization. Web. 16 April 2013. <http://www.unesco.org/new/en/social-and-human-sciences/themes/international-migration/glossary/refoulement/>.

Nozick, Robert. *Anarchy, State, and Utopia*. Cornwall: Blackwell Publishing Limited, 2001, pp. 32–3.

Othman (Abu Qatada) v. The United Kingdom, 8139/09, Council of Europe: ECHR, 17 April 2012, 56.

Saadi v. Italy, 37201/06, Council of Europe: European Court of Human Rights, 28 February 2008.

Shue, Henry. "Torture." *Philosophy and Public Affairs* 7.2 (Winter, 1978): 124-143.

Skoglund, Lena. "Diplomatic Assurances Against Torture – An Effective Strategy?" *Nordic Journal of International Law* 77.4 (2008): 319-364.

Soering v. The United Kingdom, 1/1989/161/217, Council of Europe: European Court of Human Rights, 7 July 1989.

Sussman, David. "What's Wrong With Torture?" *Philosophy and Public Affairs* 33.1 (2005): 1-33.

Waldron, Jeremy. Introduction. *Torture, Terror and Trade-Offs: Philosophy for the White House*. Oxford: Oxford University Press, 2010.

ARTICLE 6

Barnett, Michael. "Is America the Moral Leader in the World?" *CNN*. 4 July 2012. Web. 10 April 2013. <http://edition.cnn.com/2012/07/04/opinion/barnett-human-rights>.

Bellinger III, John B. "A Counterterrorism Law in Need of Updating." *The Washington Post*. 26 November 2010. Web. 10 April 2013. <http://www.washingtonpost.com/wp-dyn/content/article/2010/11/25/AR2010112503116.html>.

Chulov, Martin. "Egypt's Muslim Brotherhood Says Bin Laden Should Have Been Tried." *The Guardian*. 2 May 2011. Web. 10 April 2013. <http://www.guardian.co.uk/world/2011/may/02/egypt-muslim-brotherhood-bin-laden-tried>.

CNN Wire Staff. "World Leaders React to News of Bin Laden's Death." *CNN*. 3 May 2011. Web. 10 April 2013. <http://edition.cnn.com/2011/WORLD/asiapcf/05/02/bin.laden.world.reacts/index.html>.

"Guantanamo: In His Second Term Obama Must Correct Human Rights Failure." *Amnesty International*. 8 January 2013. Web. 10 April 2013. <https://www.amnesty.org/en/news/guant-namo-his-second-term-obama-must-correct-human-rights-failure-2013-01-08>.

"Osama Bin Laden's Death: Political Reaction in Quotes." *BBC News: US and Canada*. 3 May 2011. Web. 10 April 2013. <http://www.bbc.co.uk/news/world-us-canada-13256956>.

"Osama Bin Laden Killed: Worldwide Reactions." *The Atlantic: In Focus*. 2 May 2011. Web. 10 April 2013. <http://www.theatlantic.com/infocus/2011/05/osama-bin-laden-killed-worldwide-reactions/100058/>.

"Osama Bin Laden: More Information Needed on Circumstances of Killing." *Amnesty International*. 4 May 2011. Web. 10 April 2013. <http://www.amnesty.org.uk/news_details.asp?NewsID=19439>.

ARTICLE 8

Irvine, Derry (Lord Irvine of Lairg QC), "The Human Rights Act: Principle and Practice." *Parliamentary Affairs* 57.4 (2004): 744-753

Klug, Francesca. "A Bill of Rights: What For?" *Towards a New Constitutional Settlement*, Ed. Chris Bryant MP, The Smith Institute, 2007.

ARTICLES 9 AND 10

"Abu Hamza Among Five Terror Suspects Extradited to US." *BBC News: UK*. 6 October 2012. Web. 7 January 2013. <http://www.bbc.co.uk/news/uk-19853903>.

Casciani, Dominic. "Babar Ahmad Appeals For Trial to be Held in UK." *BBC News: UK*. 5 April 2012. Web. 17 April 2013. <http://www.bbc.co.uk/news/uk-17614935>.

Casciani, Dominic. "The Battle to Prosecute Babar Ahmad." *BBC News: UK*. 5 April 2012. Web. 17 April 2013. <http://www.bbc.co.uk/news/uk-17606337>.

"Gary McKinnon Extradition to US Blocked by Theresa May." *BBC News: UK*. 16 October 2012. Web. 7 January 2013. <http://www.bbc.co.uk/news/uk-19957138>.

Harris, Paul. "Abu Hamza and Four Other Suspects Appear in US Courts After Extradition." *The Guardian*. 6 October 2012. Web. 7 January 2013. <http://www.guardian.co.uk/world/2012/oct/06/abu-hamza-us-court-extradition1>.

Holcroft-Emmess, Natasha. “James, Wells and Lee v UK: Indefinite Detention and Arbitrary Deprivations of Liberty.” *Oxford Human Rights Hub.* 27 November 2012. Web. 7 January 2013. <http://ohrh.law.ox.ac.uk/?p=710>.

Holehouse, Matthew. “Extradition of Abu Hamza and Four Others for Terrorism Offences Can Go Ahead European Court Rules.” *The Telegraph.* 10 April 2012. Web. 7 January 2013. <http://www.telegraph.co.uk/news/uknews/terrorism-in-the-uk/9195024/Extradition-of-Abu-Hamza-and-four-others-for-terrorism-offences-can-go-ahead-European-court-rules.html>.

Kermani, Secunder. “Mahdi Hashi has British Citizenship Revoked for Extremism.” *BBC News: London.* 1 November 2012. Web. 7 January 2013.<http://www.bbc.co.uk/news/uk-england-london-20157167>.

“Mahdi Hashi has British Citizenship Revoked for Extremism.” *BBC News: London.* 3 November 2012. Web. 7 January 2013 <http://www.bbc.co.uk/news/uk-england-london-20191899>.

“The Betrayal of Mahdi Hashi.” *CagePrisoners.* 2 November 2012. Web. 7 January 2013. <http://www.cageprisoners.com/our-work/opinion-editorial/item/5276-the-betrayal-of-mahdi-hashi>.

Travis, Alan. “Two-Thirds of UK Terror Suspects Released Without Charge.” *The Guardian.* 13 May 2009. Web. 17 April 2013. <http://www.guardian.co.uk/uk/2009/may/13/terrorism-suspects-britain-uk>.

United Kingdom. *Criminal Justice Act 2003.* s225. Web. 7 January 2013.<http://www.legislation.gov.uk/ukpga/2003/44/section/225>.

Article 11

De Burca, Grainne. “The European Court of Justice and the International Legal Order After *Kadi*” *Harvard International Law Journal* 51.1 (2010): 1-50 <http://www.harvardilj.org/articles/1-50.pdf>.

Drzemczewski, Andrew. “The Sui Generis Nature of the European Convention on Human Rights” *The International and Comparative Law Quarterly* 29.1 (1980): 54-63 <http://www.jstor.org.gate2.library.lse.ac.uk/stable/758752>.

Wessel, Ramses A. “The Kadi Case: Towards a More Substantive Hierarchy in International Law?” *International Organizations Law Review* 5.2 (2008): 323-327 <http://docserver.ingentaconnect.com.gate2.library.lse.ac.uk/deliver/connect/mnp/15723739/v5n2/s4.pdf?expires=1363542333&id=73364510&titleid=11567&accname=London+School+of+Economics&checksum=EEDC7F406A4874DA3BE939E3387F86B8>.

Yassin Abdullah Kadi and Al Barakaat International Foundation v Council of the European Union and Commission of the European Communities. European Court of Justice, 3 September 2008.

Article 12

Cascani, Dominic. “Q&A: Super-injunctions.” *BBC News: UK.* 20 May 2011. Web. 17 April 2013. <http://www.bbc.co.uk/news/uk-13473070>.

Greenslade, Roy “Jimmy Savile: Why the tabloids were unable to publish and be damned.” *The Guardian.* 10 October 2012. Web. 13 March 2013. <http://www.guardian.co.uk/media/greenslade/2012/oct/10/jimmy-savile-bbc>.

Article 13

Hunt, Lynn. “Introduction.” *Inventing Human Rights: A History.* New York: W.W. Norton, 2007.

Jobs, Richard Ivan. "Youth Movements: Travel, Protest, and Europe in 1968." *The American Historical Review* 114.2 (2009): 376-404.

Slaughter, Joseph. *Human Rights, Inc.: The World Novel, Narrative Form, and International Law.* New York: Fordham University Press, 2007.

The United Nations Universal Declaration of Rights. Web. 24 April 2013. <http://www.un.org/en/documents/udhr/>.

Tuan, Yi-fu. *Space and Place: The Perspective of Experience*. Minneapolis: University of Minnesota, 1977. p52.

Weissbrodt, David S., and Connie De La. Vega. *International Human Rights Law: An Introduction*. Philadelphia: University of Pennsylvania, 2007. p71

ARTICLE 14

Kapferer, Sibylle. "Article 14(2) of the Universal Declaration of Human Rights and Exclusion from International Refugee Protection." *Refugee Survey Quarterly* 27.3 (2008): 53-75.

"Ministry of Foreign Affairs, Trade and Integration of Ecuador." *Ministry of Foreign Affairs, Trade and Integration of Ecuador*. Web. 11 April 2013. <http://www.mmrree.gob.ec/eng/2012/com042.asp>.

Quinn, Ben. "Ecuador Raises Julian Assange Case with Labour." *The Guardian*. Guardian News and Media, 29 March 2013. Web. 11 April 2013. <http://www.guardian.co.uk/media/2013/mar/30/ecuador-julian-assange-labour>.

ARTICLE 15

"Number of Syrian Refugees Reaches 1 Million Mark." *United Nations High Commissioner for Refugees*. 6 March 2013. Web. 24 April 2013. <http://www.unhcr.org/513625ed6.html>.

"Refused: The Experiences of Women Denied Asylum in the UK." *Women for Refugee Women*. Web. 25 April 2013. <http://www.refugeewomen.com/index.php/resources/publications>.

"Stories." *Women for Refugee Women*. Web. 24 April 2013. <http://www.refugeewomen.com/index.php/resources/stories>.

Syal, Rajeev. "Diane Abbott warns Labour on Immigration." *The Guardian*. 21 April 2013. Web. 25 April 2013. <http://www.guardian.co.uk/uk/2013/apr/21/diane-abbott-miliband-immigration>.

ARTICLE 16

Adams Otis, Ginger. "Swami claims Indian rape victim was 'as guilty' as her attackers." *NYDailyNews*. 7 January 2013. Web. 17 April 2013. <http://www.nydailynews.com/news/world/swami-blames-rape-victim-article-1.1234924>.

Bhowmick, Nilanjana. "The Real Shame: India's Patriarchy Roars Back After Delhi Gang Rape." *Time World*. 18 January 2013. Web. 17 April 2013.<http://world.time.com/2013/01/18/the-real-shame-indias-patriarchy-roars-back-after-delhi-gang-rape/>.

"Brazilian Economy Overtakes UK's, Says CEBR." *BBC News*.
26 December 2011. Web. 17 April 2013. <http://www.bbc.co.uk/news/business-16332115>.

Chamberlain, Gethin. "'If Girls Look Sexy, Boys Will Rape.' Is This What Indian Men Really Believe?" *The Guardian*. 23 March 2013. Web. 17 April 2013. <http://www.guardian.co.uk/world/2013/mar/24/india-rape-disturbing-attitudes-men>.

"Danger is near: 99% victims in Tamil Nadu knew their rapists." *The Times of India*. 7 January 2013. Web. 17 April 2013. <http://articles.timesofindia.indiatimes.com/2013-01-07/chennai/36191609_1_sexual-abuse-victims-sexual-assault>.

Ghose, Sagarika. "Time to Make a Choice." *Hindustan Times*.8 January 2013. Web. 17 April 2013. <http://www.hindustantimes.com/editorial-views-on/SagarikaGhose/Time-to-make-a-choice/Article1-986871.aspx> .

"Indian President Speaks out against Rape." *Al Jazeera*. 25 January 2013. Web. 17 April 2013. <http://www.aljazeera.com/news/asia/2013/01/20131251927167827 35.html>.

"India's Unwanted Girls." *BBC News*. 23 May 2011. Web. 27 April 2013. <http://www.bbc.co.uk/news/world-south-asia-13331808>.

"Justice JS Verma submits report on rape laws, 'shocked' by system's apathy" *Times of India*. 23 January 2013. Web. 17 April 2013 <http://articles.timesofindia.indiatimes.com/2013-01-23/india/36504469_1_sexual-offences-home-secretary-justice-js-verma>.

Mahr, Krista. "Another High Profile Rape in India Highlights Ongoing Problem." *World Time*. 18 March 2013. Web. 17 April 2013. <http://world.time.com/2013/03/18/another-high-profile-rape-in-india-highlights-ongoing-problem/>.

Nelson, Dean. "Men Can Still Rape Their Wives in India After New Government Bill." *The Telegraph*. 14 March 2013. Web. 17 April 2013. <http://www.telegraph.co.uk/news/worldnews/asia/india/9930838/Men-can-still-rape-their-wives-in-India-after-new-Government-bill.html>.

Schultz, Sandra and Wieland Wagner. "Rape Tragedy in India: Dreams of 'the Fearless One'." *Spiegal Online*. 25 January 2013. Web. 17 April 2013. <http://www.spiegel.de/international/world/exploring-the-lives-of-the-rape-victim-and-suspects-in-india-a-879187-2.html>.

Uttarakhand Govt. Prohibits Women from Working beyond 6 P.m." *Yahoo! News India*. 12 January 2013. Web. 17 April 2013. <http://in.news.yahoo.com/uttarakhand-govt-prohibits-women-working-beyond-6-p-075323919.html>.

"Verma Panel Submits Report on Rape Laws." *Hindustan Times*. 23 January 2013. Web. 17 April 2013. <http://www.hindustantimes.com/India-news/NewDelhi/Justice-Verma-submits-report-on-reforming-rape-laws-suggests-time-bound-trial/Article1-998567.aspx>.

ARTICLE 17

"Charter, United Nations, Chapter I, Purposes and Principles." *UN News Center*. UN. Web. 25 April 2013. <http://www.un.org/en/documents/charter/chapter1.shtml>.

Hussein Shaban, Abdul. "Human Rights: An American Weapon." *Middle East Monitor*. Web. 25 April 2013. <http://www.middleeastmonitor.com/articles/middle-east/5725-human-rights-an-american-weapon>.

ARTICLE 18 - THE CENTREPIECE OF THE UNIVERSAL DECLARATION OF HUMAN RIGHTS

Orwell, George. *1984: A Novel*. New York: Signet Classic, 1977.

Franklin, Benjamin. "Letter from Silence Dogood." The New-England Courant, Boston, Massachusetts, 1722.

In discussion with Richard Dawkins in 2009. Steven Weinberg is a Professor of Physics and Astronomy at University of Texas.

Mandela, Nelson. *Long Walk to Freedom: The Autobiography of Nelson Mandela*. Boston: Little, Brown, 1994.

ARTICLE 20

Civil Human Rights Front (Jan 2012) *A Report on the Police Abuse of Power 2011*.

European Court of Human Rights, *Plattform 'Ärzte für das Leben' v. Austria* (1991) 13 EHRR 204

Human Rights Monitor (Nov 2012) *ANNI Report 2012 on the performance of National Human Rights Institutions in Asia*

Joint Submission by NGOs coordinated by the Hong Kong Human Rights Monitor to the UN Human Rights Committee on the implementation of the ICCPR in the Hong Kong Special Administration Region, China. (Nov 2012)

Leung Kwok Hung & Others v HKSAR [2005] 3 HKLRD 164

Police Power Concern Group of Civil Human Rights Front (Nov 2012) *Decoding Public Order Ordinance: From 97 to Wolf and* Eagel. Hong Kong.

Public Order Ordinance, CAP 245.

"Record number prosecuted under tough protest law", *South China Morning Post*, 10 Nov 2012

ARTICLE 21

Harding, Luke. "Up to 28,000 Syrians Have 'disappeared' since Uprising Began." *The Guardian.* 18 October 2012. Web. 25 April 2013. <http://www.guardian.co.uk/world/2012/oct/18/28000-syrians-disappeared-uprising>.

"Kept in the Dark - The Murky World if Enforced Disappearances." *Amnesty International.* 29 August 2012. Web. 25 April 2013. <http://www.amnesty.org/en/news/kept-dark-murky-world-enforced-disappearances-2012-08-28>.
"Syria Urged to End Forced Disappearances." *Amnesty International USA.* 29 August 2012. Web. 25 April 2013. <http://www.amnestyusa.org/news/press-releases/syria-urged-to-end-enforced-disappearances-1>.

Macleod, Hugh and Annasofie Flamand. "Wave of Enforced Disappearances in Syria." *Al-Jazeera.* 24 April 2011. Web. 25 April 2013. <http://www.aljazeera.com/news/middleeast/2011/04/2011424201513361740.html>.

"Syria Conflict: William Hague to Meet Opposition Leaders." *BBC News: Politics.* 15 November 2012. Web. 25 April 2013. <http://www.bbc.co.uk/news/uk-politics-20335346>.

"Syria Civil War 'Kills 36,000'." *The Telegraph.* 31 October 2012. Web. 25 April 2013. <http://www.telegraph.co.uk/news/worldnews/middleeast/syria/9645076/Syria-civil-war-kills-36000.html>.

ARTICLE 22

Dickens, Charles. *Hard Times.* Oxford: Oxford University Press, 2008.

ARTICLE 23

'Woman Work', by Maya Angelou. Available at http://allpoetry.com/poem/8511443-Woman_Work-by-Maya_Angelou.

ARTICLE 24

Barford, Vanessa. "Should People be Off on Fridays?" *BBC News: Magazine.* 1 February 2013. Web. 25 April 2013. <http://www.bbc.co.uk/news/magazine-21242782>.

Boyle, David. "Keynes and the Treasury." *New Economics.* 24 June 2010. Web. 25 April 2013. <http://www.neweconomics.org/blog%20?page=116&iframe=true&width=100%25&height=100%25>.

"Brits Want 4 Day Week." *YouGov.* Web. 28 February 2013.<http://yougov.co.uk/news/2013/02/28/brits-want-4-day-week/>.

"Costs and Benefits." *Global Workplace Analysis.* Web. 25 April 2013. <http://www.teleworkresearchnetwork.com/resources/costs-benefits>.

Hours of Work: From Fixed to Flexible? (Rep) International Labour Organization. Web. 25 April 2013. <http://www.ilo.org/public/english/standards/relm/ilc/ilc93/pdf/rep-iii-1b.pdf>.

"Poverty Overview." *World Bank.* Web. 25 April 2013. <http://www.worldbank.org/en/topic/poverty/overview>.

Price, Ian. "Four-day Working Week? Three Cheers!" *The Guardian.* 16 April 2011.Web. 25 April 2013. <http://www.guardian.co.uk/money/2011/apr/16/four-day-working-week>.

"Work Time" *International Labour Organization.* Web. 25 April 2013. <http://www.ilo.org/global/standards/subjects-covered-by-international-labour-standards/working-time/lang--en/>.

"Yahya Jammeh Gives Gambians An Extra Day Off." *BBC News: Africa.* 1 February 2013. Web. 25 April 2013. <http://www.bbc.co.uk/news/world-africa-21280766>.

Article 25

Firmin, Carlene. "Female Genital Mutilation: The UK Must Act Now." *The Guardian.* 26 March 2013. Web. 25 April 2013.<http://www.guardian.co.uk/society/2013/mar/26/female-genital-mutilation-preventive-approach>.

Ford, Liz. "UK Funds Aim to End Female Genital Mutilation 'in a Generation'." *The Guardian.* 6 March 2013. Web. 26 March 2013. <http://www.guardian.co.uk/global-development/2013/mar/06/uk-funds-female-genital-mutilation-generation>.

"Midwife 'Role' as NHS Targets Female Genital Mutilation." *BBC News: UK.* 2 February 2013. Web. 26 March 2013. <http://www.bbc.co.uk/news/uk-21306861>.

UN Women, "United Nations Bans Female Genital Mutilation." *UN Nations.* 20 December 2012. Web. 26 March 2013. <http://www.unwomen.org/2012/12/united-nations-bans-female-genital-mutilation/>.

United Kingdom. Department for International Development. *A Time For Change: Ending Female Genital Mutilation.* 22 March 2013. Web. 26 March 2013. <https://www.gov.uk/government/case-studies/a-time-for-change-ending-female-genital-mutilation>.

United Kingdom. Hansard, Commons Debates: *Justice: Female Genital Mutilation: Prosecutions.* 3 November 2010. Web. 26 March 2013. <http://www.publications.parliament.uk/pa/cm201011/cmhansrd/cm101103/text/101103w0002.htm>.

United Kingdom. Home Office. *Policy: Ending Violence Against Women and Girls in the UK*. Web. 26 March 2013. <https://www.gov.uk/government/policies/ending-violence-against-women-and-girls-in-the-uk>.

Article 27

Constanides, Panos. "The Development and Consequences of New Information Infrastructures: The Case of Mashup Platforms." *Media, Culture and Society.* 34.5 (2012): 606-622.

Goldacre, Ben. "Bad Pharma: How Drug Companies Mislead Doctors and Harm Patients." 2012. London: Fourth Estate. pp. 56-59.

Spence, Michael. "The Justification of Intellectual Property." *Intellectual Property,* 2007. Oxford: Oxford University Press. pp 46 - 52.

Article 28

"An AK-47 - Often The 'Credit Card' For FARDC Soldiers." *Amnesty International.* Web. 25 April 2013. <http://www2.amnesty.org.uk/blogs/press-release-me-let-me-go/ak-47-often-credit-card-fardc-soldiers>.

"Former Sudan Child Soldier Emmanuel Jal to Speak Out on Global Arms Trade Treaty with Amnesty International Media Tour March 5-7 in New York and Washington, D.C." *Amnesty International USA.* 25

February 2013. Web. 25 April 2013. <http://www.amnestyusa.org/news/press-releases/former-sudan-child-soldier-emmanuel-jal-to-speak-out-on-global-arms-trade-treaty-with-amnesty-intern>.

Naidoo, Kumi. "Two Bullets per Person: The Trillion Dollar Military Spending Club." Web log post. 17 April 2012. Web. 25 April 2013. <http://www.greenpeace.org/international/en/news/Blogs/makingwaves/two-bullets-per-person-the-trillion-dollar-mi/blog/40000/>.

"Peacekeeping Budgets and Personnel Soar to New Heights." *Worldwatch Institute.* Web. 25 April 2013. <http://www.worldwatch.org/node/5466>.

"Shattered Lives: The Case For Tough International Arms Control." *Control Arms.* Web. 25 April 2013. <http://controlarms.org/wordpress/wp-content/uploads/2011/02/Shattered-lives-the-case-for-tough-international-arms-control.pdf> .

ARTICLE 29

Cho, Jong Ik. "Tourist Internet Cut After a Month." *Daily NK.* 29 March 2013. Web. 25 April 2013. <http://www.dailynk.com/english/read.php?cataId=nk00100&num=10448>.

Green, Chris. "2% of North Koreans Now Use Orascom." *Daily NK.* 19 April 2011. Web. 25 April 2013. <http://www.dailynk.com/english/read.php?cataId=nk00100&num=7589>.

Park, Seong Guk. "Koryolink Mobile Internet Launched." *Daily NK.* 26 February 2013. Web. 25 April 2013. <http://www.dailynk.com/english/read.php?cataId=nk00100&num=10345>.

Seo, Yoon Hwan. "Whither Information Freedom in 'Reforming' NK?" *Daily NK.* 13 September 2013. Web. 25 April 2013. <http://www.dailynk.com/english/read.php?cataId=nk03600&num=9787>.

ARTICLE 30

Herzog, Werner. *Death Row.* Channel 4. 22 March 2012, 29 March 2013 and Thursday 5 April 2013. Television.

McDonald, Sir Trevor. *Inside Death Row With Trevor McDonald.* ITV. 17 January 2013 and 24 January 2013. Television.

* 9 7 8 1 7 8 0 3 5 6 3 8 9 *

ND - #0148 - 080726 - C4 - 297/210/4 - PB - 9781780356389 - Gloss Lamination